LIVERPOOL CITY CENTRE

HISTORY TOUR

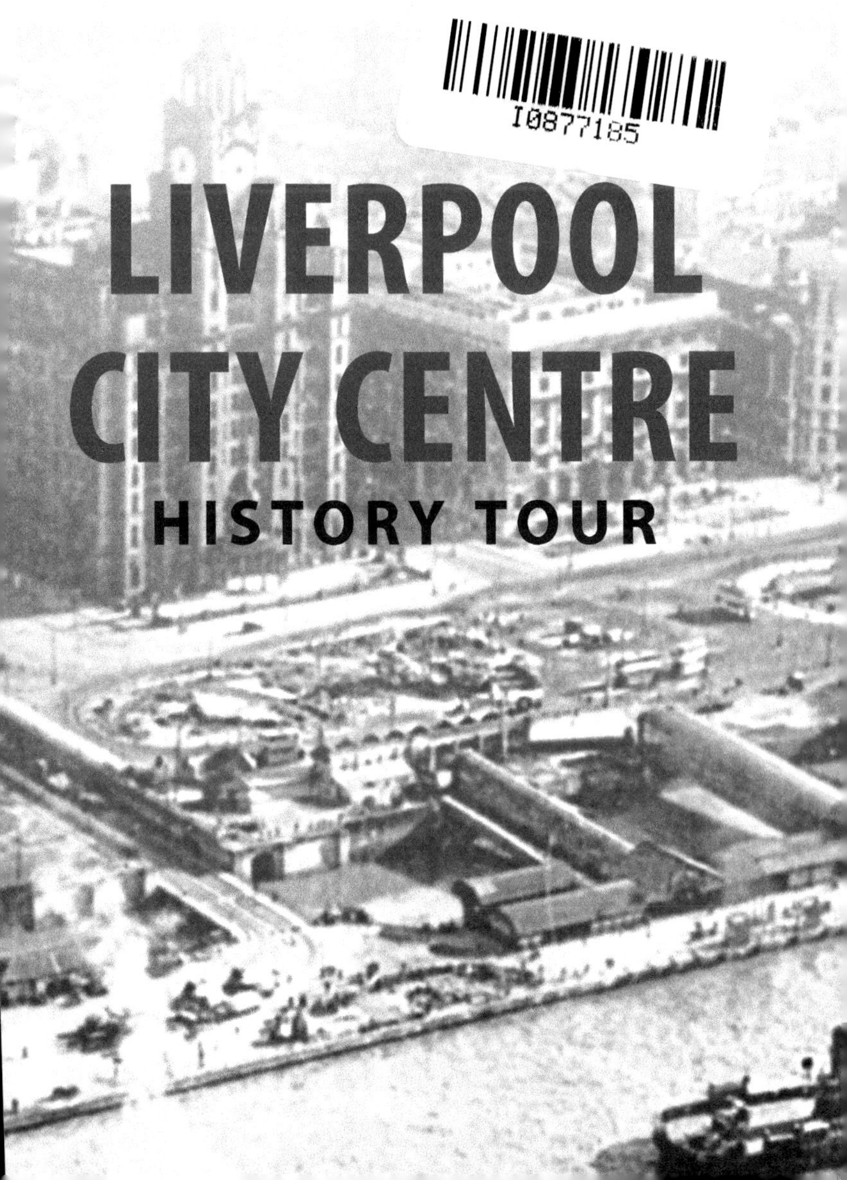

First published 2017

Amberley Publishing
The Hill, Stroud,
Gloucestershire, GL5 4EP
www.amberley-books.com

ISBN 978 1 4456 6666 2 (print)
ISBN 978 1 4456 6667 9 (ebook)

British Library Cataloguing in Publication Data.
A catalogue record for this book is available from the British Library.

Origination by Amberley Publishing.
Printed in Great Britain.

INTRODUCTION

It was at the end of the seventeenth century that the trade to America began to expand with the importation of West Indian sugar and Virginia tobacco and the increase in the exports of Lancashire textiles. The coalfields were developed across Lancashire and this was exported through Liverpool. Sugar refineries, salt and glass works, metal crafts and potteries were established in the town and Cheshire rock salt was exported through the port.

In 1698, the town had twenty-four streets and the population increased from 6,000 to 20,000 in 1750, and 80,000 in 1800. The number of ships using the port increased from 102 in 1700 to 4,746 in 1800 and land was developed creating Hanover Street, Park Lane and Duke Street. Williamson Square, Clayton Square, Cleveland Square, Wolstenholme Square and St Paul's Square were all completed. The Bluecoat School for orphan boys was opened in 1708, the Royal Infirmary between 1745 and 1749 and the Seamen's Hospital in 1752. The Town Hall was constructed between 1749 and 1754, and was reconstructed in 1795 following a serious fire that damaged the building.

The population of the city in 1895 was 503,967, increasing to 685,276 by 1901. The following year the districts of Garston, Aigburth and Allerton, extending 1,673 acres, with a population of 17,288, were annexed. In 1903 the population was around 717,000, and the area of the city 14,909 acres. Bootle was granted a charter as an independent borough in 1868 and in 1895 Walton, Wavertree, West Derby and Toxteth became part of Liverpool.

Garston was added in 1902, Fazakerley in 1905, Allerton, Childwall, Little Woolton and Much Woolton in 1913, the remainder of West Derby and Croxteth in 1928 and Speke in 1932. Liverpool was granted city status by royal charter in 1880, when it also became the seat of a new diocese that included part of Chester and south-west Lancashire. The Roman Catholic Church had made Liverpool the seat of a diocese in 1850 and two great cathedrals were built in the city in the twentieth century.

The city of Liverpool has changed dramatically in the last 100 years, but the majority of the buildings in the city centre were constructed in Victorian times and still retain their charm and distinctive character. It is a city steeped in history but one that is also looking forward to its rightful place in modern Britain. It is the country's second largest port and has been the major gateway for people arriving from Northern and Southern Ireland.

Liverpool celebrated its 800th anniversary in 2007 and became European Capital of Culture the following year. The city centre has been transformed in the last few years by the opening of the new Liverpool One shopping development. Grosvenor's £1-billion project provides retail, leisure, residential facilities and office accommodation. It includes the provision of large department stores, hotels, cinema, cafés, restaurants, bars and a new bus station. There are further plans to regenerate the city centre to ensure that it remains as one of the major tourist, commercial and business centres of the North West of England.

The city has over 2,500 listed buildings, of which twenty-seven are Grade I listed and eighty-five are Grade II listed. It has a greater number of public sculptures than any other in the United Kingdom, aside from Westminster, and more Georgian houses than the city of Bath. It has been described by English Heritage as England's finest Victorian city even though many of the buildings were lost during the Blitz and sustained German bombing during the Second World War.

KEY

1. Waterloo Dock Warehouse
2. Riverside Station
3. Royal Liver Buildings
4. Cunard Building
5. Port of Liverpool Building
6. The New Museum of Liverpool
7. Albert Dock
8. Dock Traffic Office
9. Custom House
10. The Liverpool Overhead Railway
11. Georges Dock Ventilation and Control Station
12. Albion House
13. Victoria Monument
14. Bank of England Building
15. National Westminster Bank
16. India Buildings
17. Tower Building
18. Church of Our Lady and St Nicholas
19. Oriel Chambers
20. Martins Bank Head Office
21. Liverpool Town Hall
22. Liverpool, London and Globe Building
23. Cotton Exchange
24. Liverpool Exchange Station
25. Royal Insurance Building
26. General Post Office
27. Magistrates' Court
28. The Tramways Building
29. The Mersey Tunnel
30. William Brown Library and Museum
31. Walker Art Gallery
32. County Sessions House
33. St John's Gardens
34. St George's Hall
35. North Western Hotel
36. Lime Street Station
37. Blacklers
38. St Peter's Church, Church Street
39. Liverpool Blue Coat School
40. Lewis's
41. St Peter's Church, Seel Street
42. Central Hall
43. No. 62 Rodney Street
44. Liverpool Anglican Cathedral
45. Liverpool Philharmonic Hall
46. Liverpool Metropolitan Cathedral
47. University of Liverpool

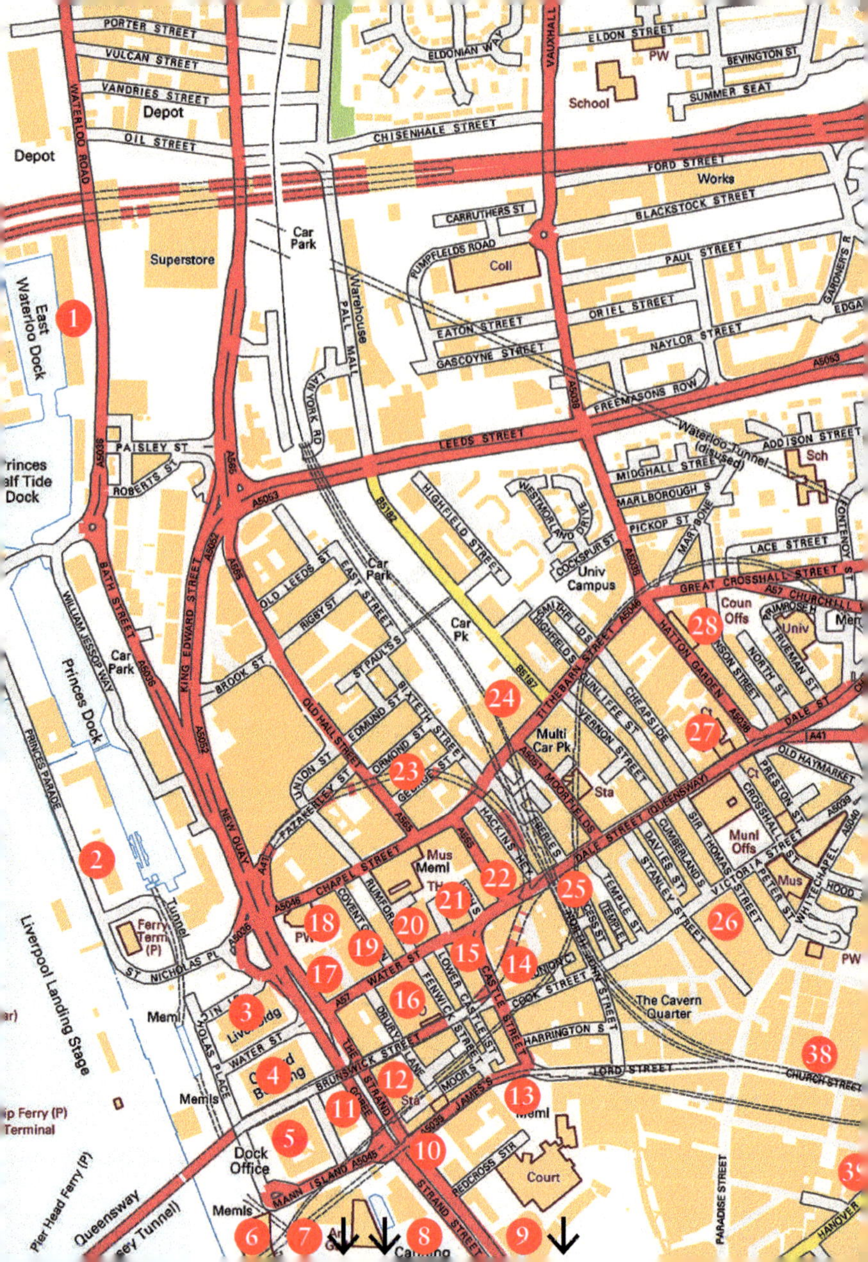

PORTER STREET
VULCAN STREET
VANDRIES STREET
Depot
OIL STREET
Depot
WATERLOO ROAD
ELDONIAN WAY
VAUXHALL
ELDON STREET
PW
BEVINGTON ST
School
SUMMER SEAT
CHISENHALE STREET
FORD STREET
Works
BLACKSTOCK STREET
CARRUTHERS ST
PUMPFIELDS ROAD
Coll
Car Park
Superstore
East Waterloo Dock
PAUL STREET
ORIEL STREET
EATON STREET
GASCOYNE STREET
NAYLOR STREET
Warehouse
PALL MALL
LANYORK RD
FREEMASONS ROW
LEEDS STREET
Waterloo Tunnel (disused)
ADDISON STREET
Sch
MIDGHALL STREET
MARLBOROUGH S
PICKOP ST
PAISLEY ST
ROBERTS ST
A5053
Princes Half Tide Dock
HIGHFIELD STREET
WESTMORLAND DRIVE
COCKSPUR ST
Univ Campus
LACE STREET
GREAT CROSSHALL STREET
Coun Offs
Univ
OLD LEEDS ST
RIGBY ST
EAST STREET
Car Park
Car Pk
BATH STREET
KING EDWARD STREET
WILLIAM JESSOP WAY
Car Park
Princes Dock
BROOK ST
ST PAUL'S S
HATTON GARDEN
NORTH ST
TRUEMAN ST
TITHEBARN STREET
Multi Car Pk
CHEAPSIDE
VERNON STREET
DALE ST
OLD HAYMARKET
PRINCES PARADE
OLD HALL STREET
EDMUND ST
ORMOND ST
UNION ST
FAZAKERLEY ST
NEW QUAY
MOORFIELDS
Sta
PRESTON ST
CROSSHALL ST
Muni Offs
DALE STREET (QUEENSWAY)
HACKINS HEY
CHAPEL STREET
Mus
Memi
SIR THOMAS STREET
VICTORIA STREET
Mus
WHITECHAPEL
HOOD
Liverpool Landing Stage
Ferry Term (P)
Tunnel
ST NICHOLAS PL
COVENT G
RUMFORD
WATER ST
FENWICK
LOWER CASTLE ST
CASTLE STREET
NORTH JOHN STREET
STANLEY STREET
TEMPLE ST
PW
COOK STREET
The Cavern Quarter
Memi
Liver Bldg
WATER ST
HARRINGTON S
DRURY LANE
BRUNSWICK STREET
LORD STREET
CHURCH STREET
THE STRAND
GOREE
MOORS
JAMES S
Sta
Memi
Memls
Pier Head Ferry (P) Terminal
Dock Office
MANN ISLAND
A5036
REDCROSS STR
Court
PARADISE STREET
HANOVER
Pier Head Ferry (P)
Queensway
Memls
STRAND STREET
1
2
3
4
5
6
7
8
9
10
11
12
13
14
15
16
17
18
19
20
21
22
23
24
25
26
27
28
38

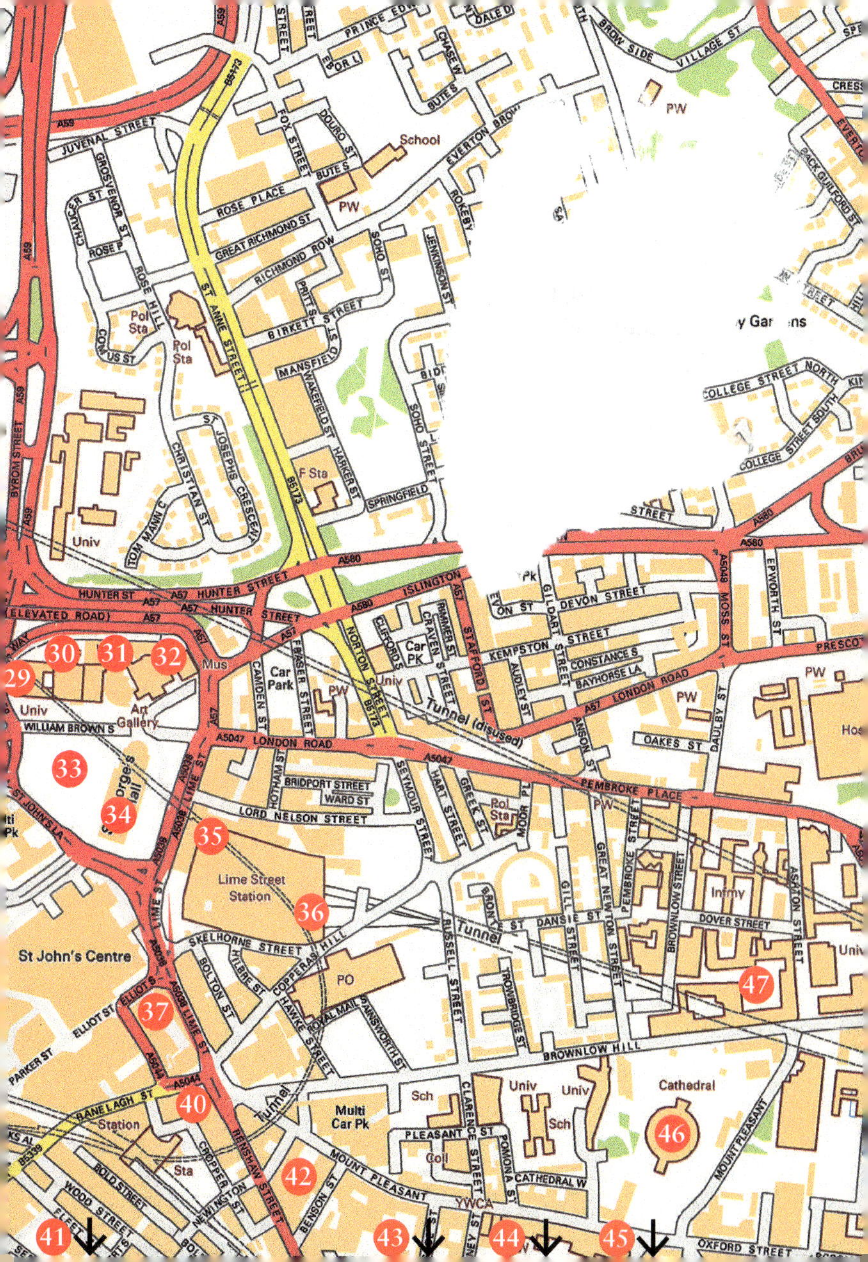

A59
B5173
PRINCE EDW
DALE D
BROW SIDE
VILLAGE ST
PW
CRESS
JUVENAL STREET
A59
FOX STREET
DOURO ST
School
BUTE S
EVERTON BROW
CHASE W
ROSE PLACE
GREAT RICHMOND ST
RICHMOND ROW
PW
SOHO ST
JENKINSON ST
ROKEBY
CHAUCER ST
GROSVENOR ST
ROSE P
ROSE HILL
Pol Sta
Pol Sta
COMUS ST
ST ANNE STREET
BIRKETT STREET
PRITT S
MANSFIELD
WAKEFIELD ST
HARKER ST
SOHO STREET
y Gar ns
COLLEGE STREET NORTH
COLLEGE STREET SOUTH
COLLEGE
ST JOSEPHS CRESCENT
CHRISTIAN ST
TOM MANN C
BYROM STREET
F Sta
B5173
SPRINGFIELD
STREET
A580
Univ
HUNTER ST
A57
HUNTER STREET
A580
ISLINGTON
A57
ELEVATED ROAD
A57
HUNTER
STREET
A580
DEVON STREET
GILDART STREET
A5049
MOSS ST
EPWORTH ST
PRESCOT
KEMPSTON STREET
CONSTANCE S
BAYHORSE LA
LONDON ROAD
A57
PW
PW
CLIFFORD S
RIMMER ST
CRAVEN STREET
STAFFORD ST
AUDLEY ST
Car PK
Car Park
CAMDEN ST
FRASER STREET
NORTON STREET
B5173
Univ
Tunnel (disused)
ANSON ST
DAULBY ST
OAKES ST
Mus
Art Gallery
Univ
WILLIAM BROWN S
A5047
LONDON ROAD
A5047
PEMBROKE PLACE
HOTHAM ST
BRIDPORT STREET
WARD ST
LORD NELSON STREET
SEYMOUR STREET
HART STREET
GREEK ST
Pol Sta
MOOR PL
PW
PEMBROKE STREET
GREAT NEWTON STREET
ST JOHN'S LA
A5038
LIME ST
Lime Street Station
BRONTE ST
GILL STREET
DANSIE ST
Tunnel
BROWNLOW STREET
Infmy
DOVER STREET
ASHTON STREET
Univ
St John's Centre
SKELHORNE STREET
COPPERAS HILL
BOLTON ST
HILBRE ST
PO
RUSSELL STREET
TROWBRIDGE ST
HAWKE STREET
ROYAL MAIL ST
SAINSWORTH ST
ELLIOT S
ELLIOT ST
PARKER ST
A5038 LIME ST
BROWNLOW HILL
Cathedral
A5044
RANELAGH ST
B5339
Station
Sta
CROPPER ST
RENSHAW STREET
Tunnel
Multi Car Pk
Sch
PLEASANT ST
CLARENCE STREET
POMONA ST
Univ
Univ
Sch
MOUNT PLEASANT
Coll
CATHEDRAL W
YWCA
MOUNT PLEASANT
BOLD STREET
WOOD STREET
FLEET ST
NEWINGTON ST
BENSON ST
OXFORD STREET
29
30
31
32
33
34
35
36
37
40
41
42
43
44
45
46
47

1. WATERLOO DOCK WAREHOUSE

The warehouses at Waterloo Dock are almost identical to those at Albert Dock. Waterloo Dock warehouse now incorporates approximately 114 apartments. Located close to the Pier Head, this warehouse conversion has much of its original features with its exposed brick, original cast-iron supporting columns, full-length windows and vaulted, barrelled ceilings. The dock was designed by Jesse Hartley and was opened in 1834.

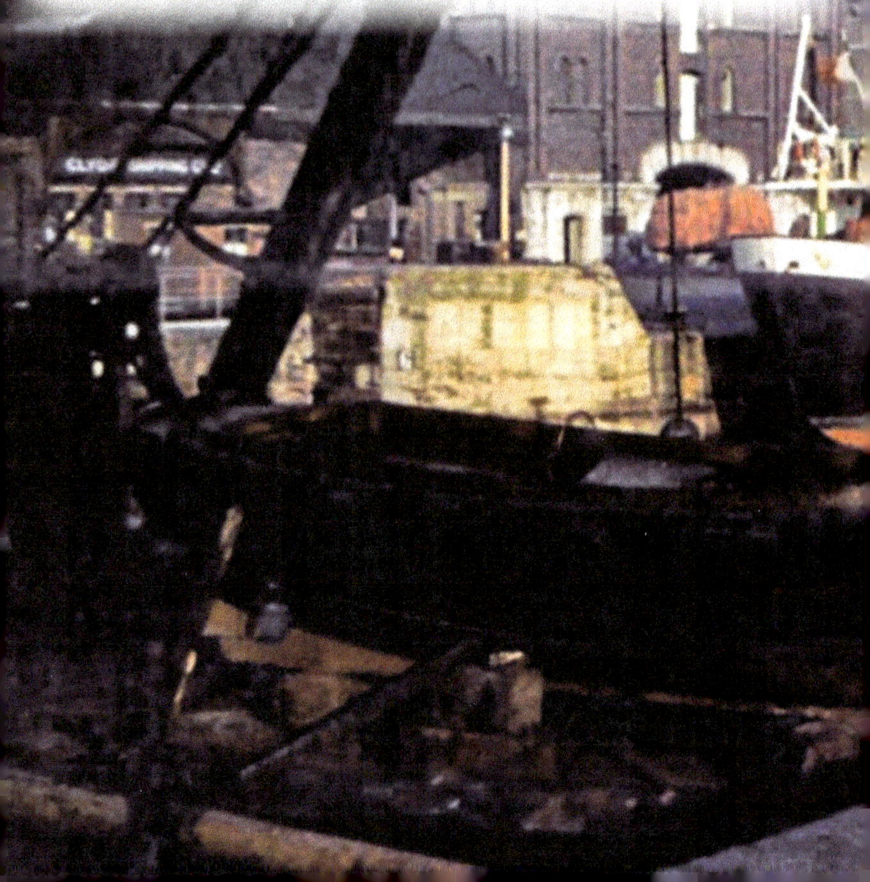

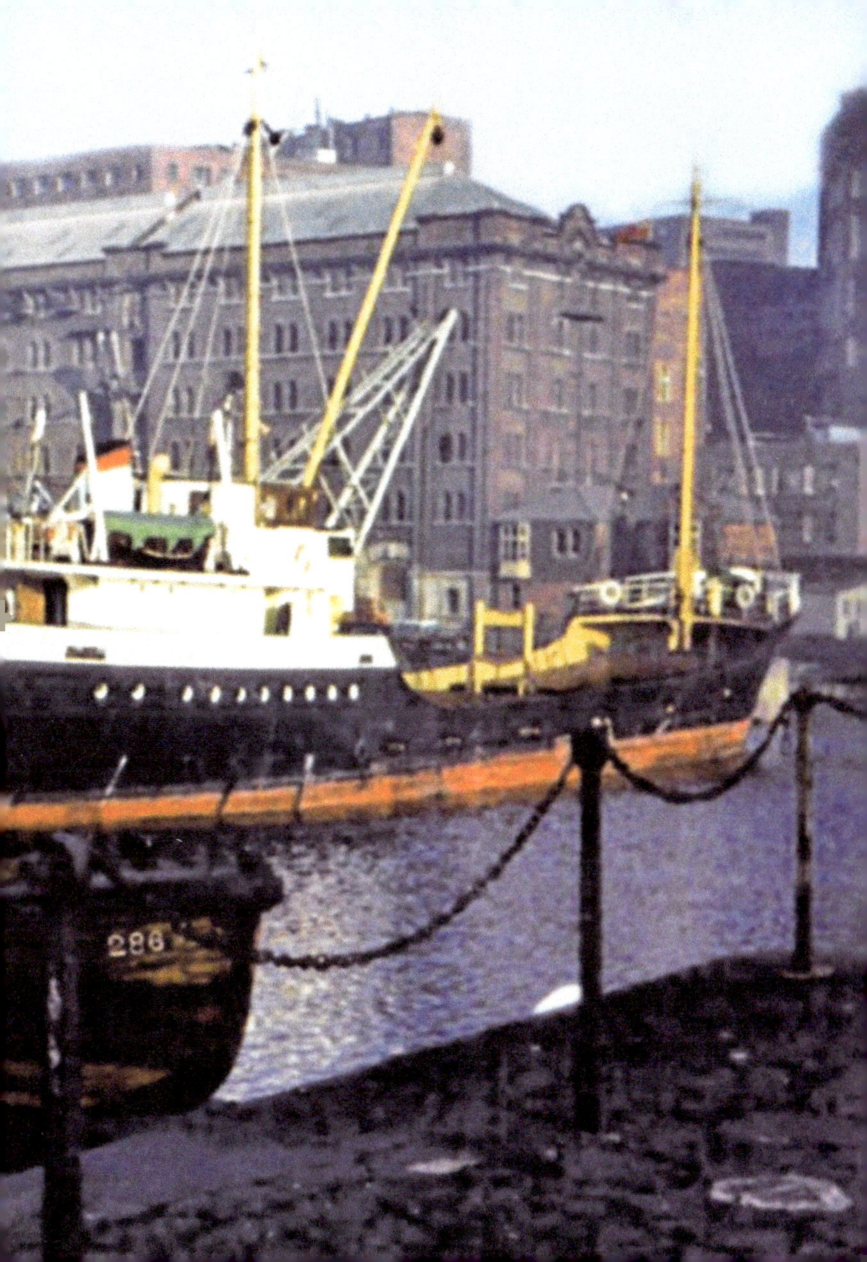
286

2. RIVERSIDE STATION

At the Pier Head, the station was opened on 12 June 1895 and was used to allow passengers to travel to the ocean liners by rail. It had two main platforms of 795 feet and 698 feet, with a centre release track between them and a 560-foot bay platform covered by a roof. Beyond the buffers were waiting rooms and an inspector's office. The last train to use the station was a troop train carrying soldiers bound for Belfast on 25 February 1971, and it was demolished in the 1990s.

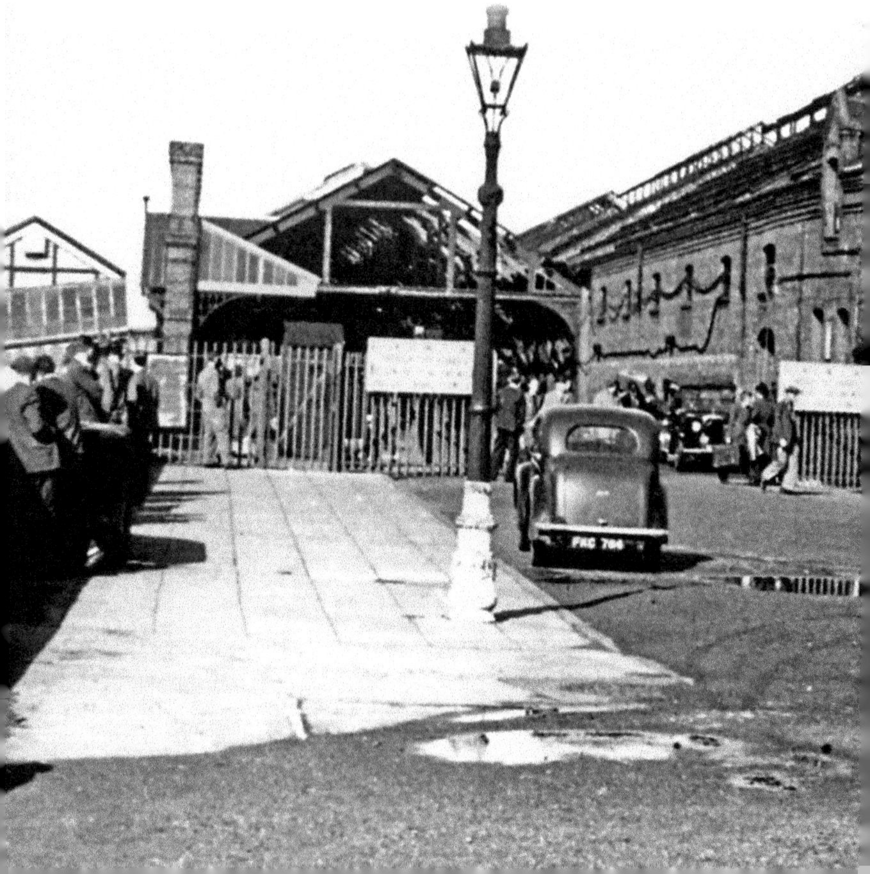

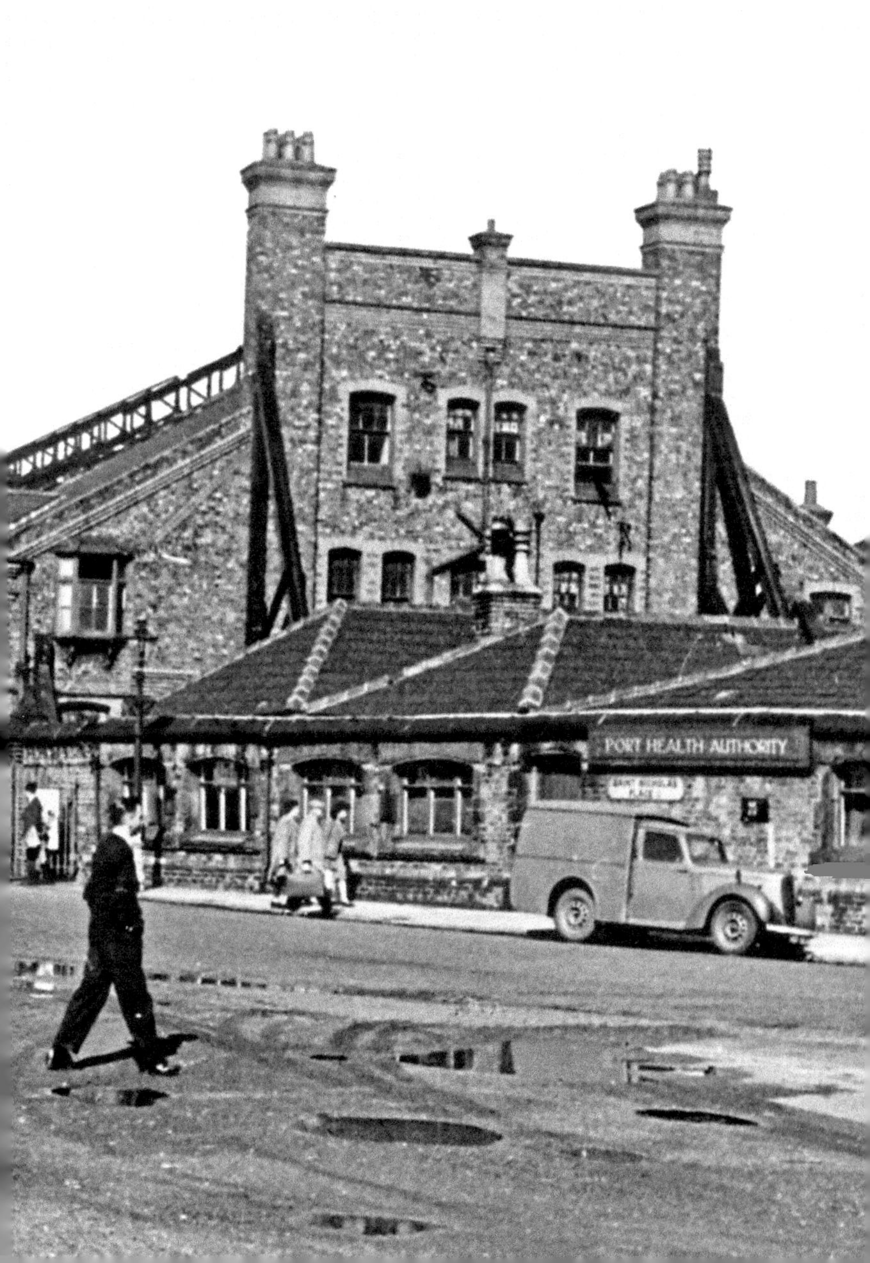
PORT HEALTH AUTHORITY

3. ROYAL LIVER BUILDINGS

The building was officially opened by Lord Sheffield on 19 July 1911 and was also constructed using reinforced concrete faced with granite. The building incorporates two clock towers and the clock faces are 25 feet in diameter, which are larger than those on Big Ben in London and were the largest electronically driven clocks in Britain. The clocks were originally called George clocks as they were started at the exact time that George V was crowned on 22 June 1911; electronic chimes were added in 1953. The building is 301 feet long, 178 feet wide, 170 feet high to the main roof and 295 feet to the top of the main towers. The Liver Birds, designed by Carl Bernard Bartels, stand at the top of each tower, with one bird looking over the city and the other facing the river. Legend says that if one of the birds were to fly away then Liverpool would cease to exist.

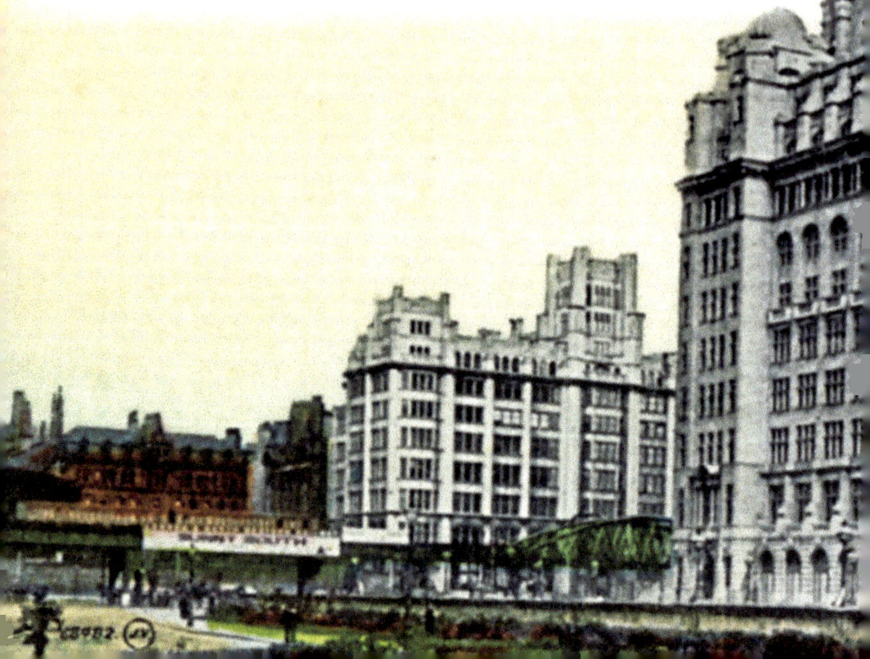

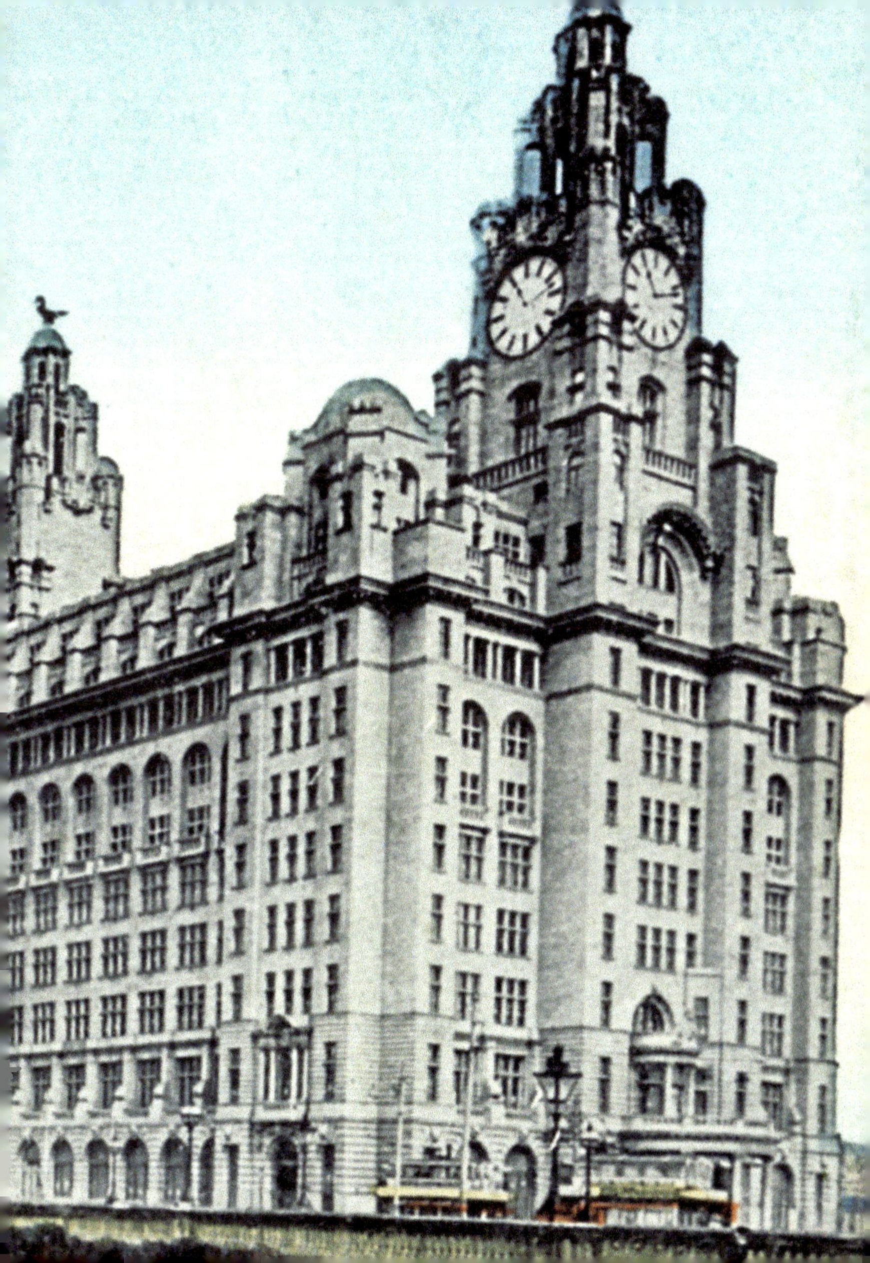

4. CUNARD BUILDING

The building was the headquarters of the Cunard Line, which became the Cunard White Star Line in 1934. It incorporated a large booking hall on the ground floor with models of some of the passenger liners that had been conceived, designed and planned in the building, such as the *Queen Mary* and *Queen Elizabeth*. Incorporated in the building was space for waiting rooms for first-, second- and third-class passengers, luggage storage rooms and a currency exchange. The basement became an air-raid shelter during the Second World War and was the central Air Raid Precautions headquarters for the city of Liverpool.

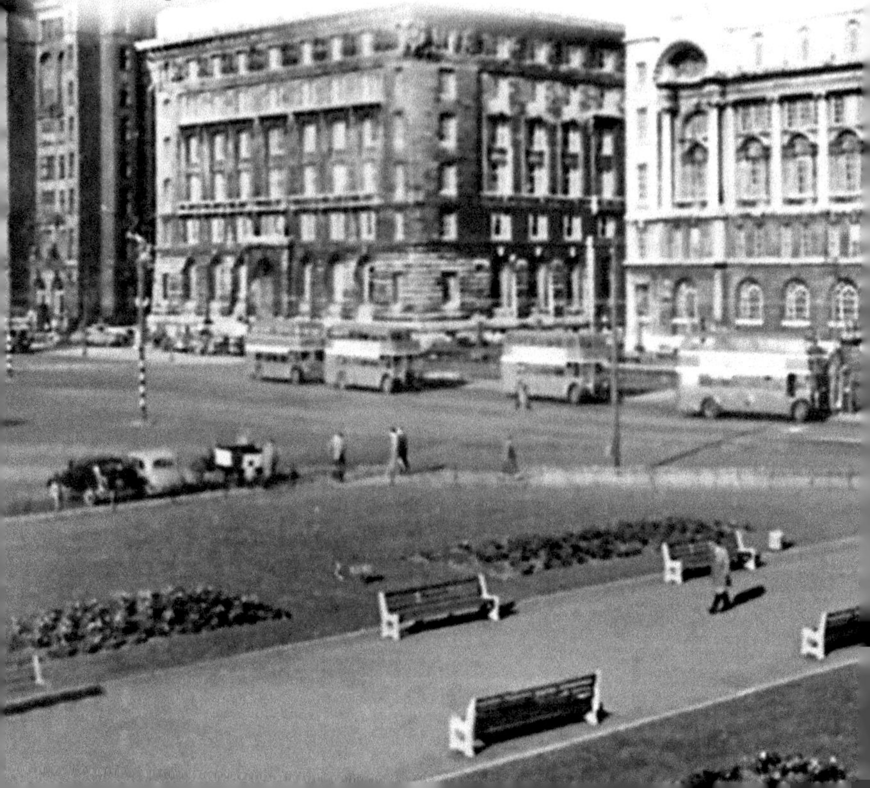

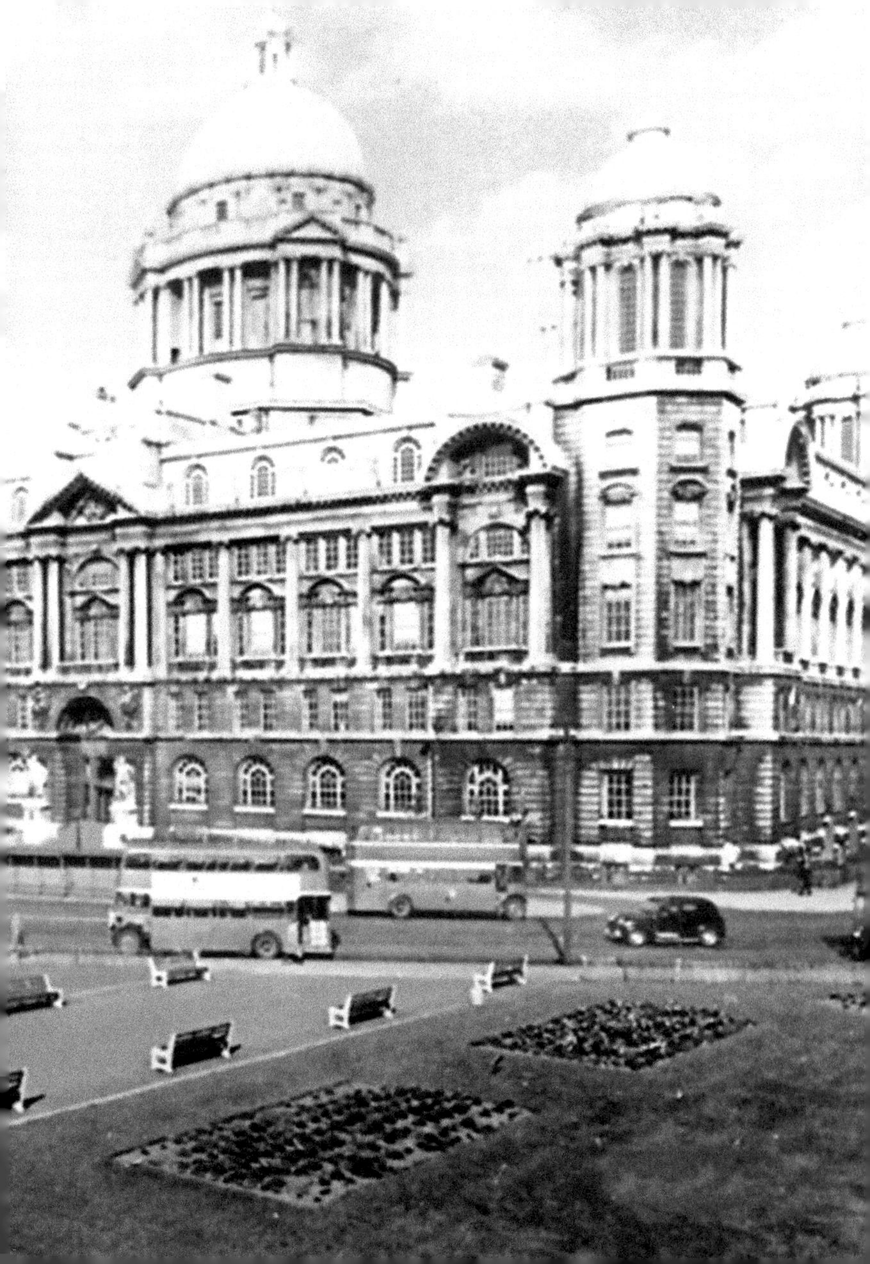

5. PORT OF LIVERPOOL BUILDING

The water was run out of Georges Dock in 1900 and Sir Arnold Thornley and F. B. Hobbs were given the job of designing a headquarters building for the Mersey Docks and Harbour Board. Work on the 'dock offices' began in 1904 and the building was completed in 1907 at a cost of £350,000. It was built with a reinforced concrete frame and is clad in Portland stone and was designed in Edwardian baroque style with a large dome on top. The fact that it was built using reinforced concrete meant that it was not only structurally strong but it was also more fire resistant than other buildings. As it was built on the site of the old dock, it also required deeper than normal foundations and over 35,000 tons of cement was used. Also, as it was built next to the river, asphalt was used to coat the floors and walls of the basement to ensure that it was waterproof.

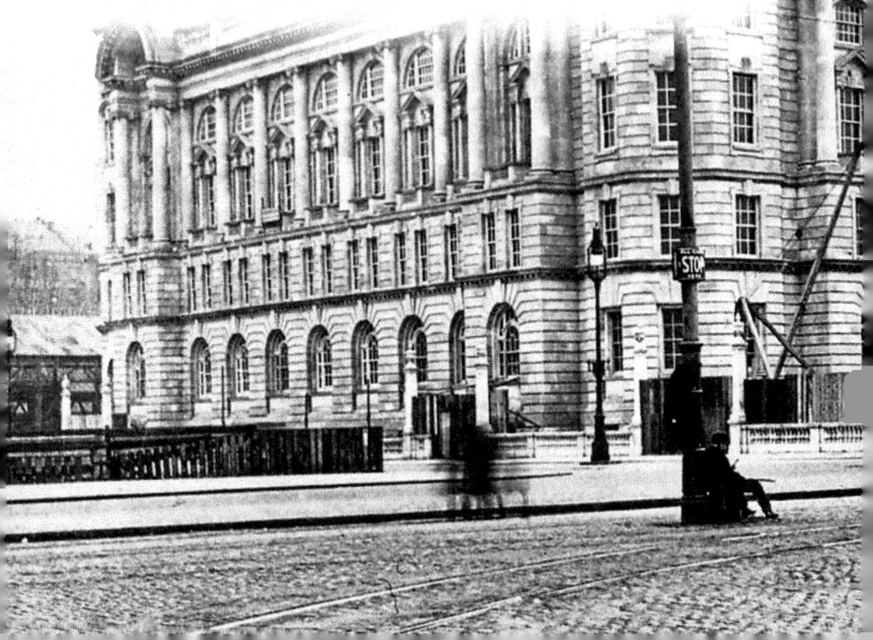

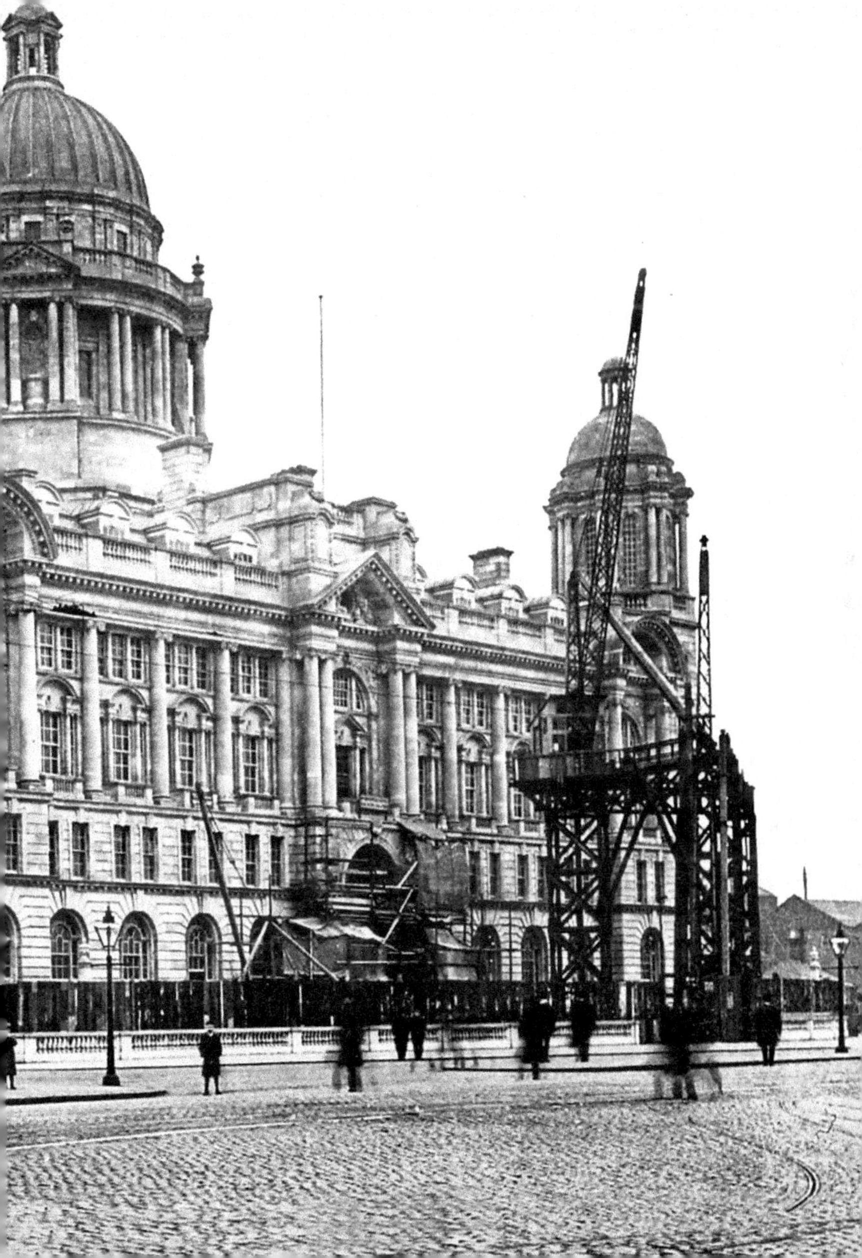

6. THE NEW MUSEUM OF LIVERPOOL

The New Museum of Liverpool at the Pier Head is part of the National Museums of Liverpool group. The building was opened on 19 July 2011, replacing the former Museum of Liverpool Life, and was built to reflect the city's global significance through its unique geography, history and culture. It is situated in a new purpose-built building at Mann Island. The story of Liverpool life is told through collections of costumes and decorative art, entomological and botanical collections and objects representing social and economic history, archaeological items and photographic images.

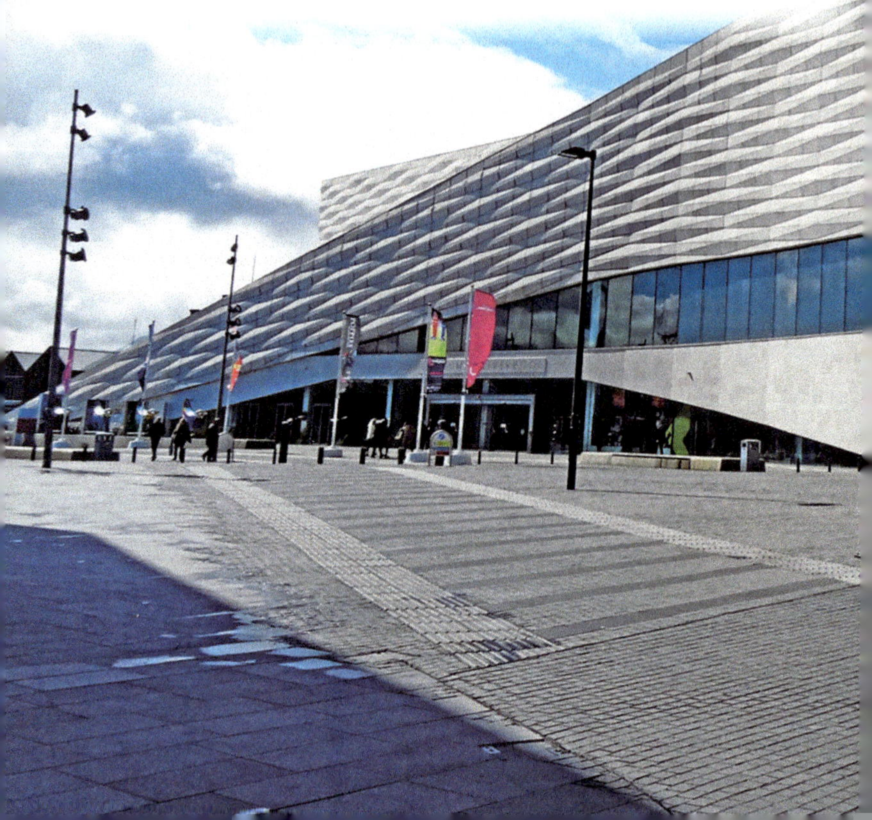

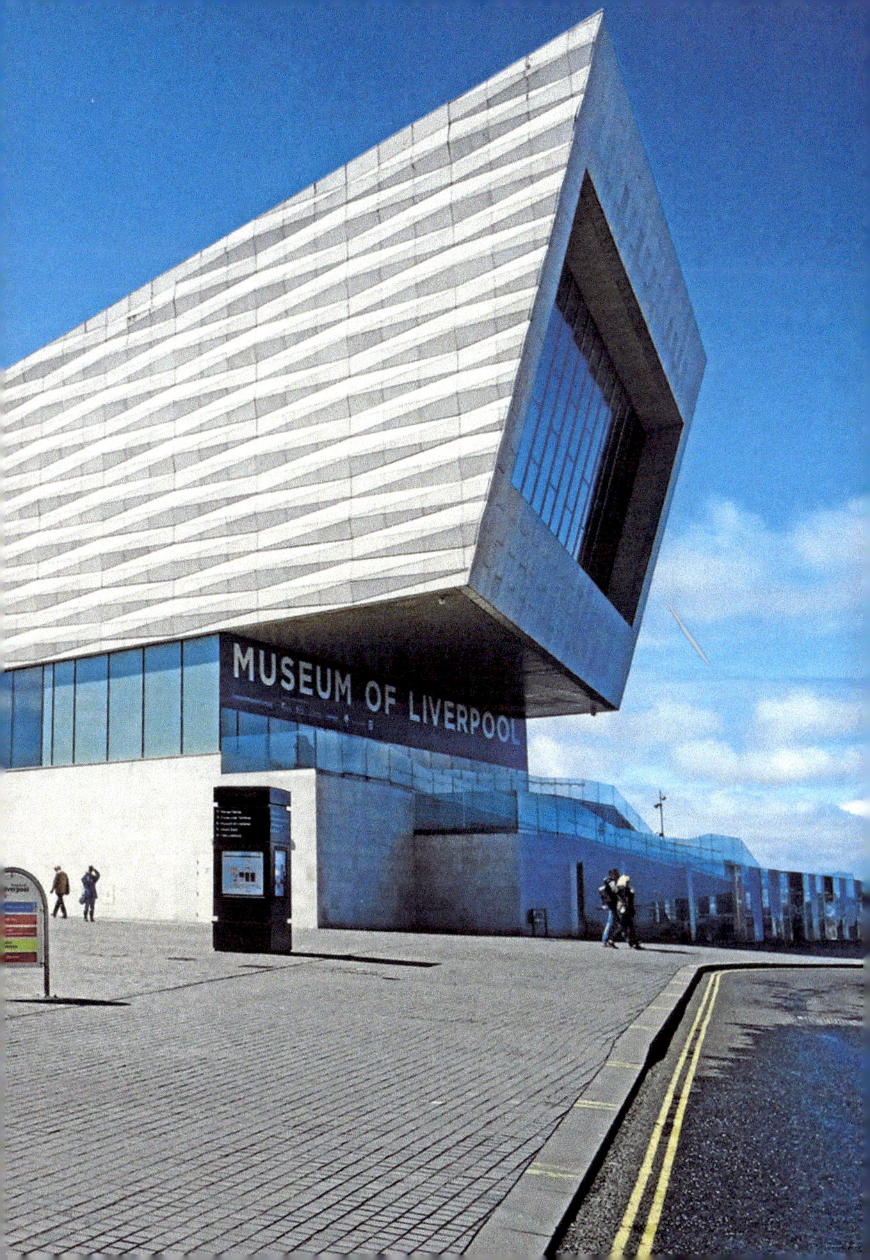
MUSEUM OF LIVERPOOL

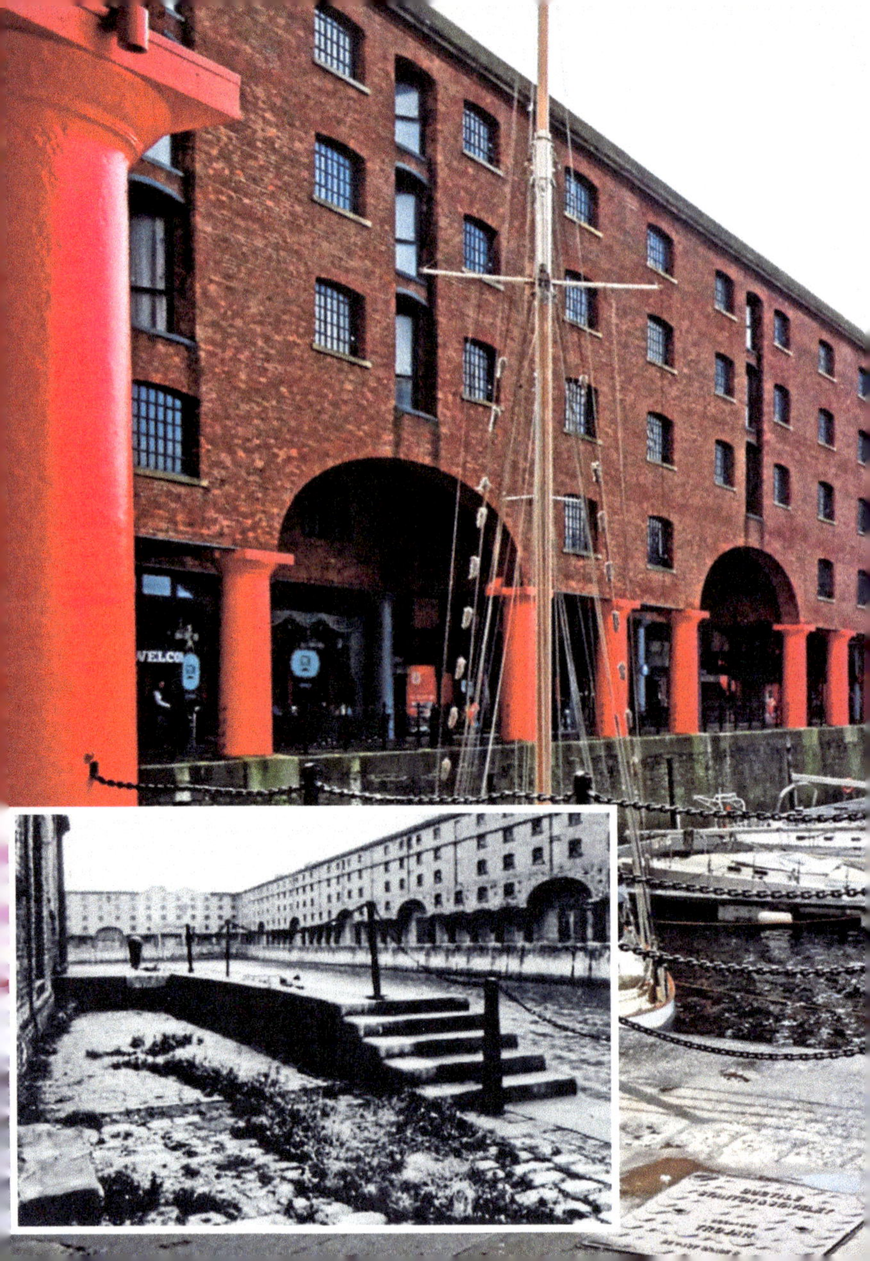

7. ALBERT DOCK

Albert Dock was designed by Jesse Hartley and Philip Hardwick and was opened in 1846 by Prince Albert. This was the first time that a member of the royal family had made a state visit to the city. The warehouse complex was the first structure in Britain to be built of cast iron, stone and brick with no wood included in the building. Goods were loaded and unloaded directly to the warehouses and items such as brandy, tobacco, ivory cotton, silk, tea and sugar were kept in the secure stores. The dock was not completed until 1847; a new Dock Traffic Office was constructed the following year and the first hydraulic cargo handling hoist system was installed. In 1983, Arrowcroft Plc and the Merseyside Development Corporation signed a contract creating the Albert Dock Company. The Merseyside Maritime Museum opened at the dock in 1986 and Albert Dock was officially opened by Prince Charles two years later.

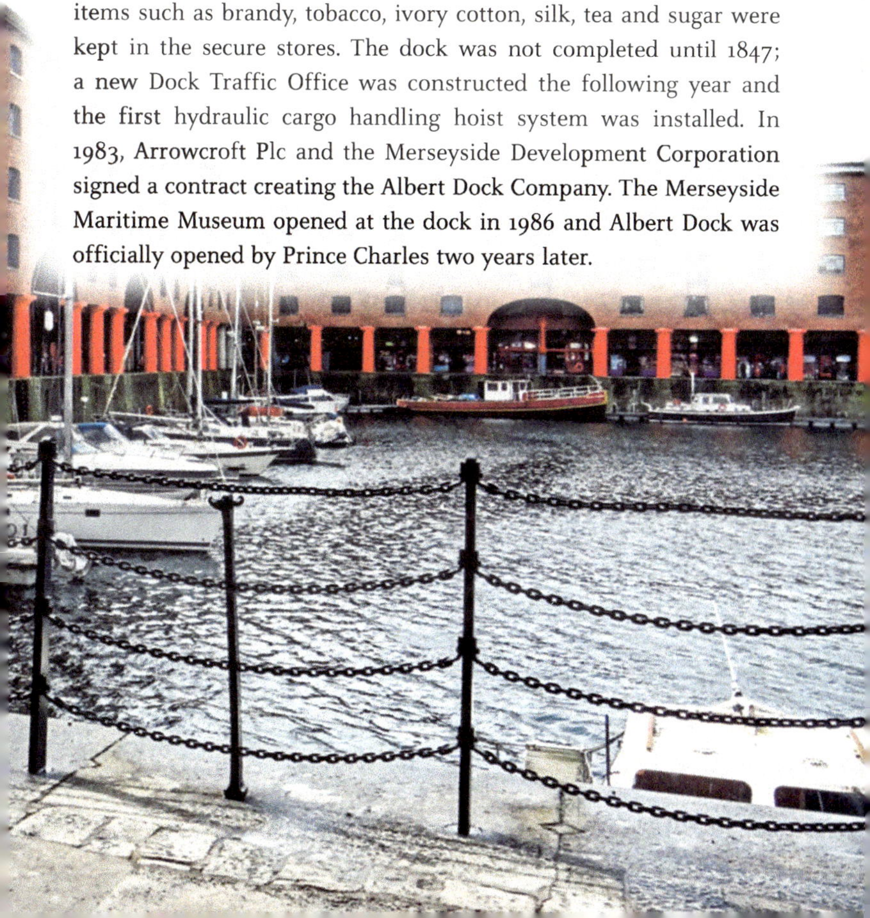

8. DOCK TRAFFIC OFFICE

The Dock Traffic Office at Albert Dock was built in 1847 and was designed by Philip Hardwick. The top story of the building was added by Jesse Hartley. It is built of brick with red sandstone dressings and has prominent battered chimney stacks with connecting arches. There is a cast-iron Tuscan portico and frieze with four columns that are 3.5 metres high with a diameter of 1 metre at the base and were cast in two halves and brazed together along their length. In 1984, after many years of neglect, the building was restored and used as television news studios for a short time by Granada Television. Four years later a new national morning television show, *This Morning*, moved to London in 1996, and in March 2003 it was announced that Granada would close its base at the Dock Office as a cost-cutting measure following its merger with the Carlton Group.

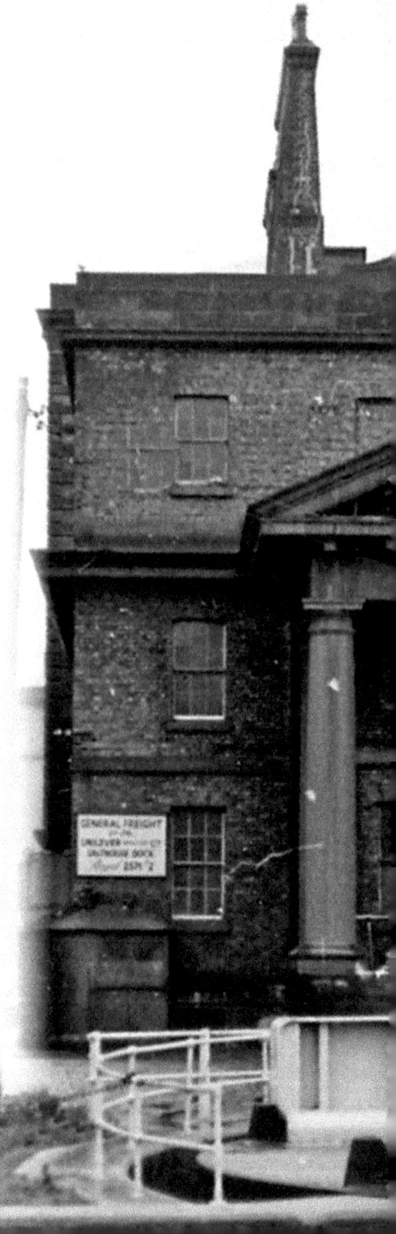

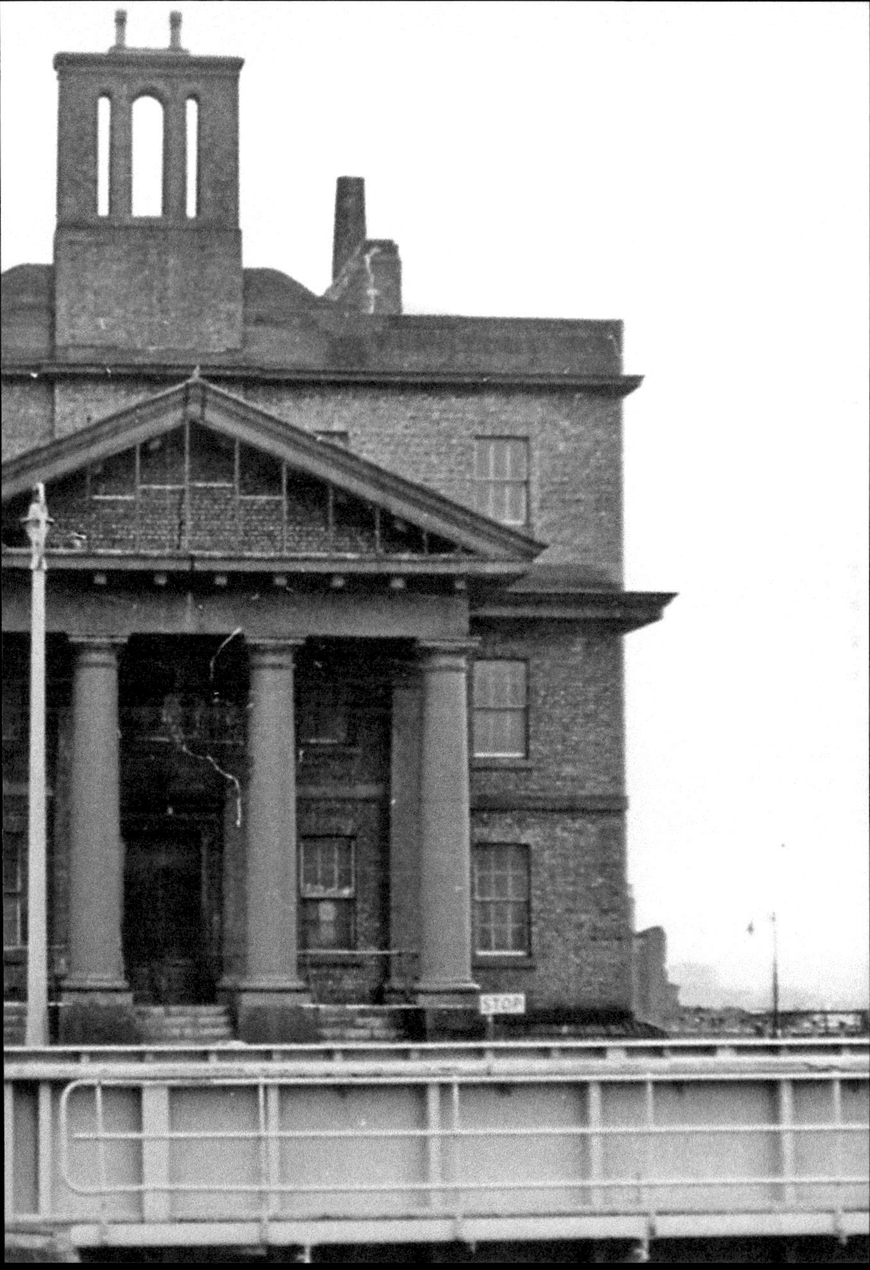
STOP

9. CUSTOM HOUSE

The Customs House was built between 1828 and 1839 and was designed by John Foster on the site of the Old Dock. It incorporated a post office, a telegraph office and offices for the Mersey Docks and Harbour Board. The local newspaper reported that, 'people gasped as the knight in shining armour came galloping into view, waving a sword as his horse pranced over the cobbles.' This was the king's champion, who had been summoned to make a traditional appearance to celebrate George IV's birthday on 12 August 1828. The day was marked by the construction of Liverpool's new Custom House. The Custom House was bombed on the night of 3/4 May 1941 in the Blitz and the decision to demolish the building was one of the most contested actions made by the city council.

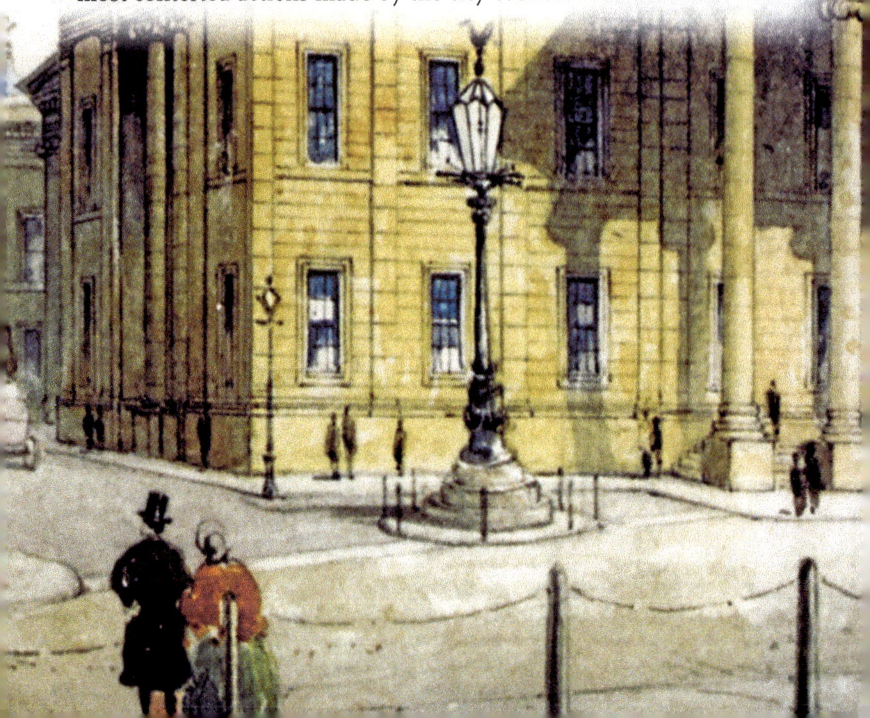

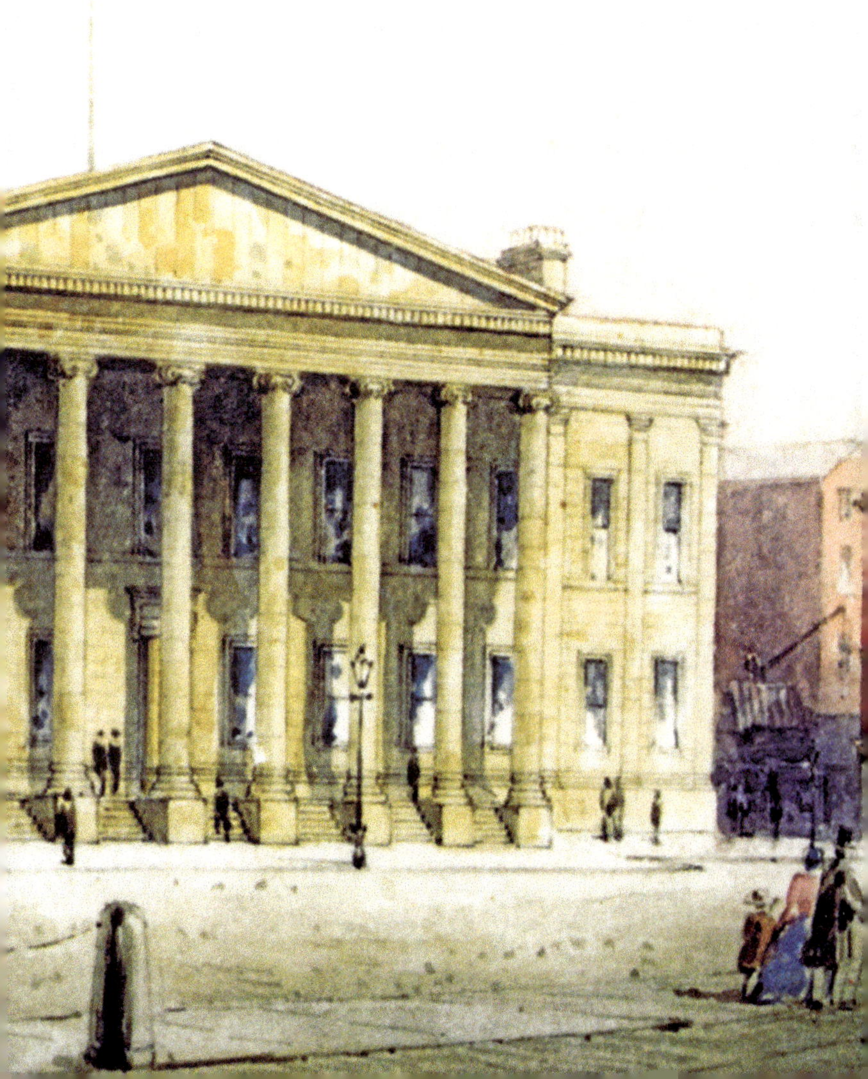

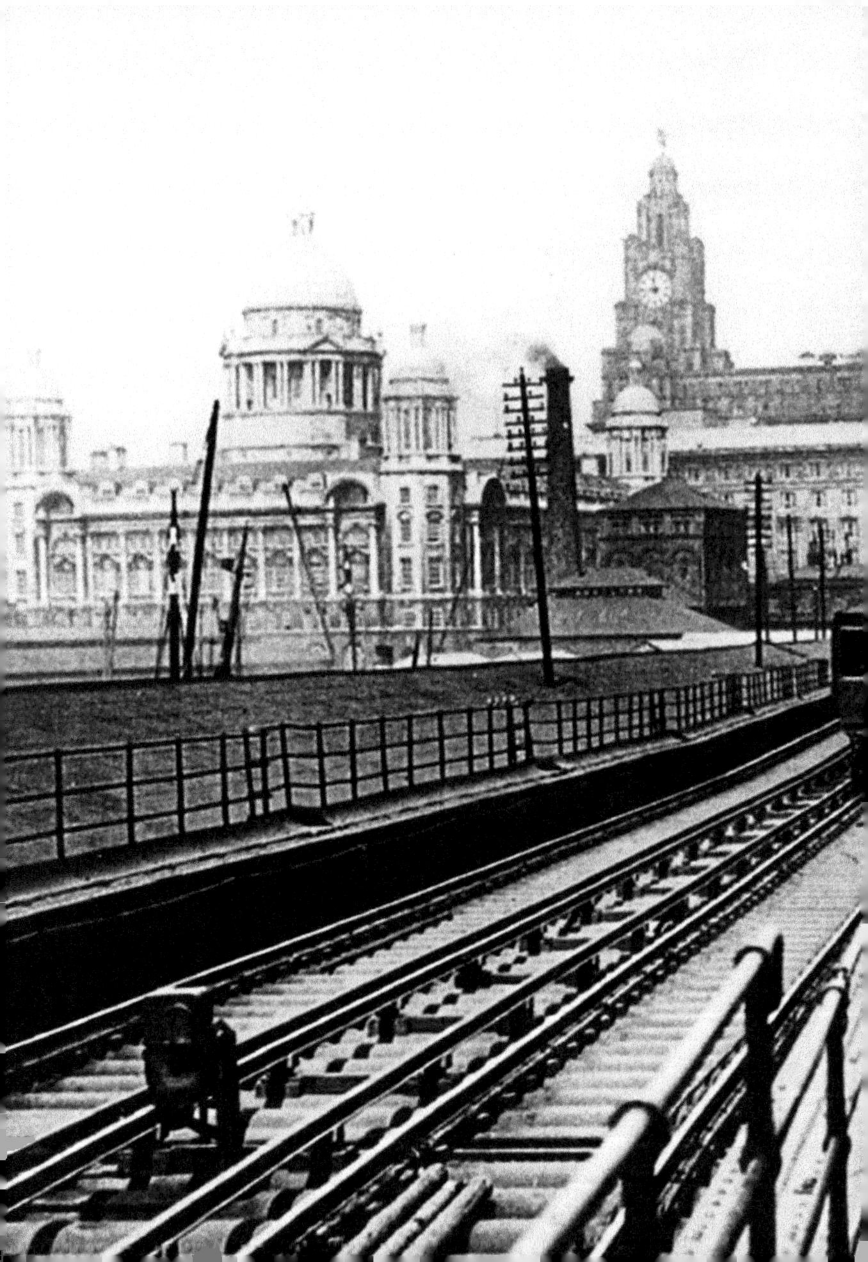

10. THE LIVERPOOL OVERHEAD RAILWAY

Located at the rear of the Royal Liver Building, the railway was the world's first electrically operated overhead railway and ran from Dingle to Seaforth along Dock Road. It was opened on 4 February 1893 by the Marquis of Salisbury and ran for 6 miles from Alexandra Dock to Herculaneum, with eleven stations along the line. It was extended to Seaforth Sands on 30 April 1894 and to Dingle on 21 December 1896. A northward extension was completed in 1905, which took the line to the tracks to the Lancashire and Yorkshire Railway's North Mersey branch, allowing a service to be provided to Aintree Racecourse when the Grand National Race took place. The railway suffered bomb damage during the Second World War and it was not nationalised in 1948. The Overhead Railway closed on 30 December 1956. Work to completely demolish the line commenced in 1957 and was completed the following year.

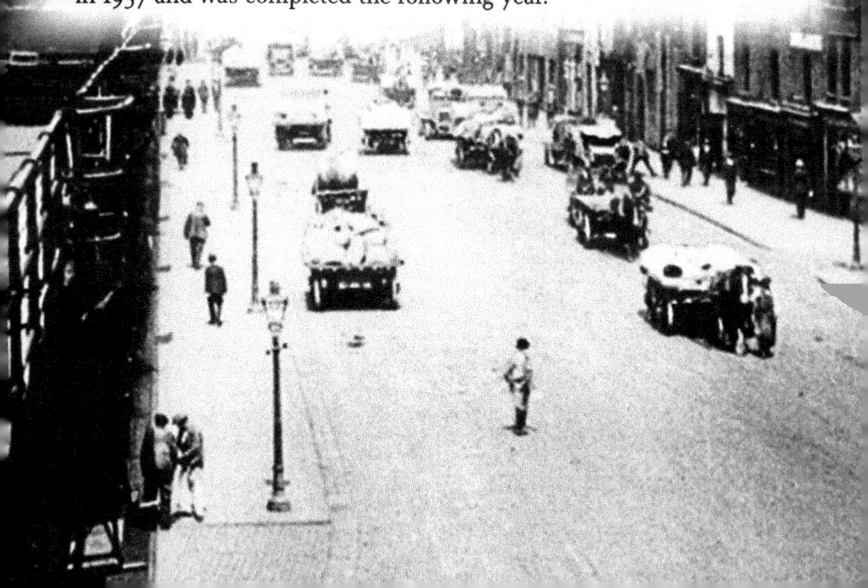

11. GEORGES DOCK VENTILATION AND CONTROL STATION

The George's Dock Ventilation and Control Station contain offices and 3 metre diameter blade fans that extract air and force air back to ventilate the Birkenhead Queensway Tunnel. It is Portland stone faced and has sculptures by Edmund C. Thompson, assisted by George T. Capstick. The building was built in art deco style, symbolising the motor car in 1931–34 and was designed by Herbert J. Rowse, with engineers Sir Basil Mott and J. A. Brodie.

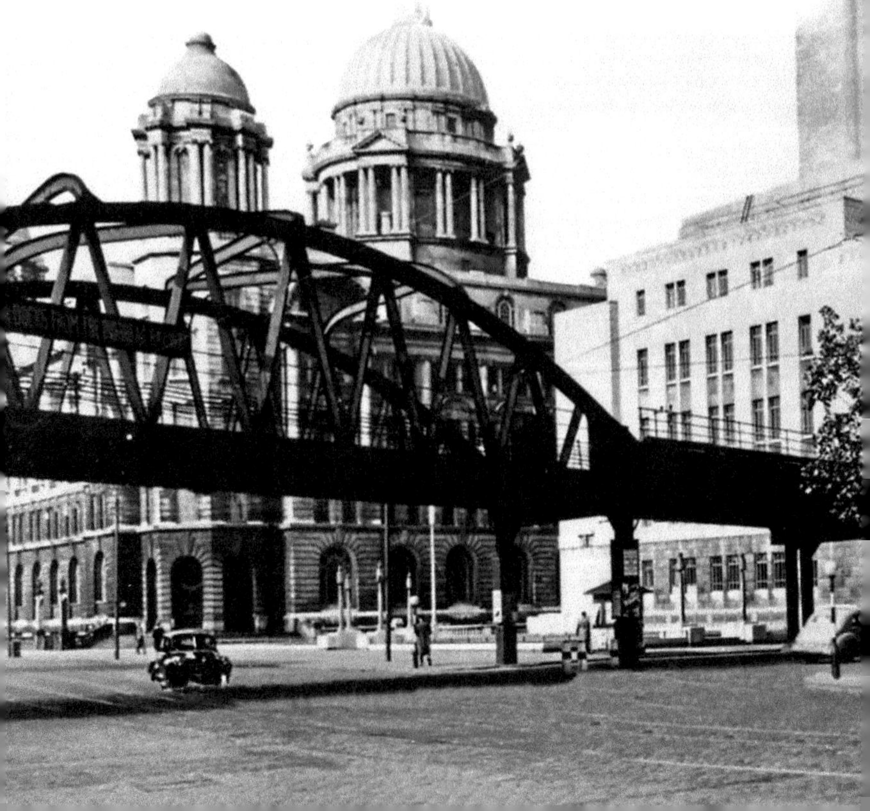

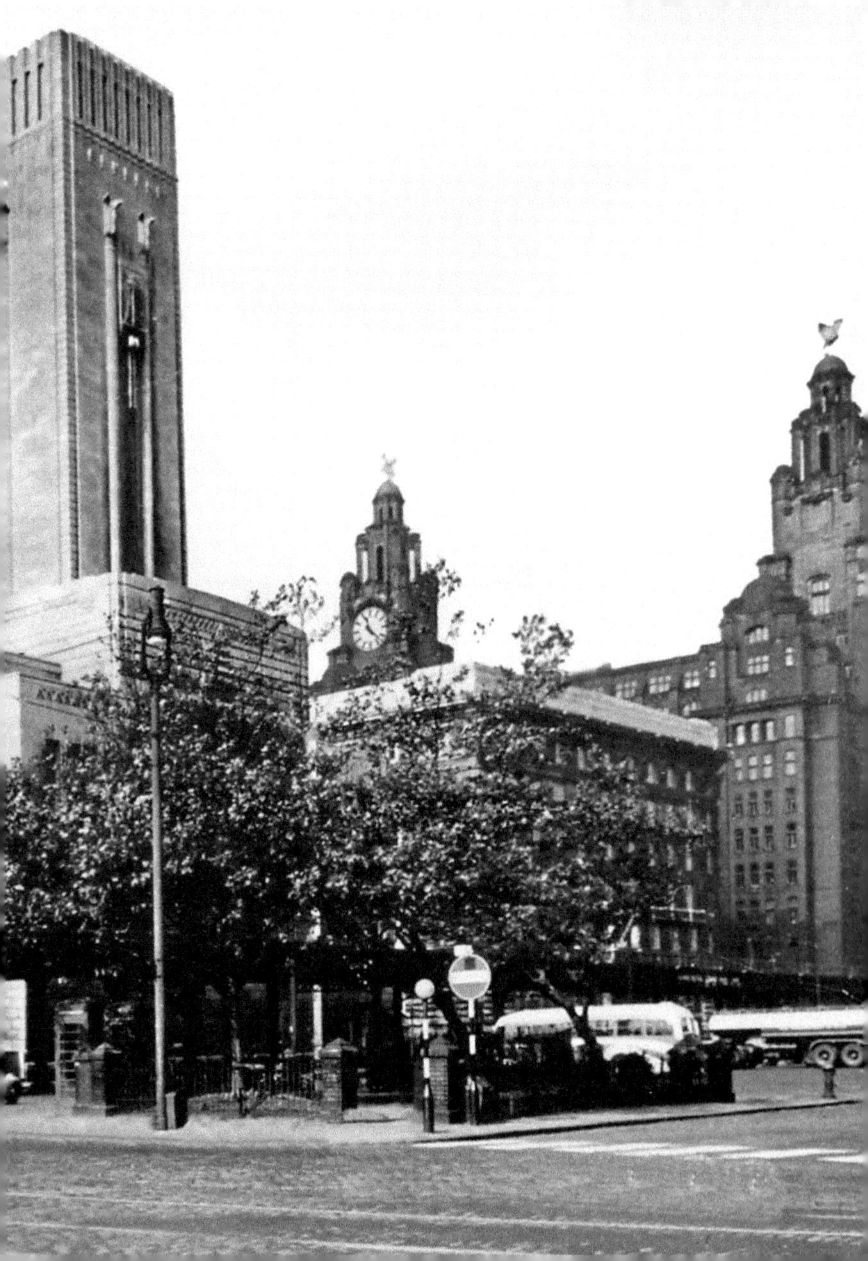

12. ALBION HOUSE

Albion House was built in 1898 for Ismay, Imrie & Co., otherwise known as the White Star Line, and is a Grade II-listed building. The building was designed by Norman Shaw and J. Francis Doyle. It is situated at the corner of The Strand and James Street, and is constructed from white Portland stone and red brick, similar to the former New Scotland Yard building in London. After several years of dereliction, the building was purchased in 2014 and converted to a luxury Titanic-themed hotel at a cost of £5.5 million.

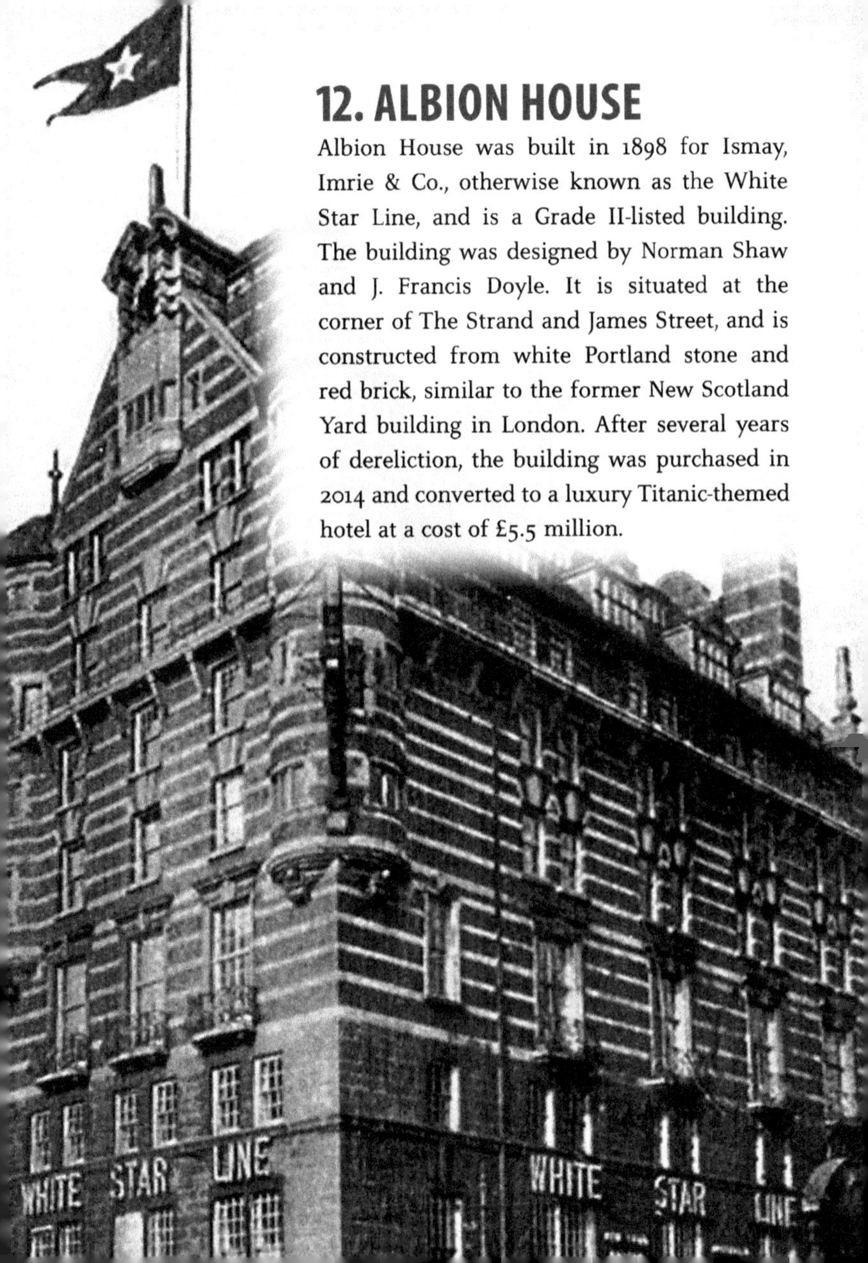

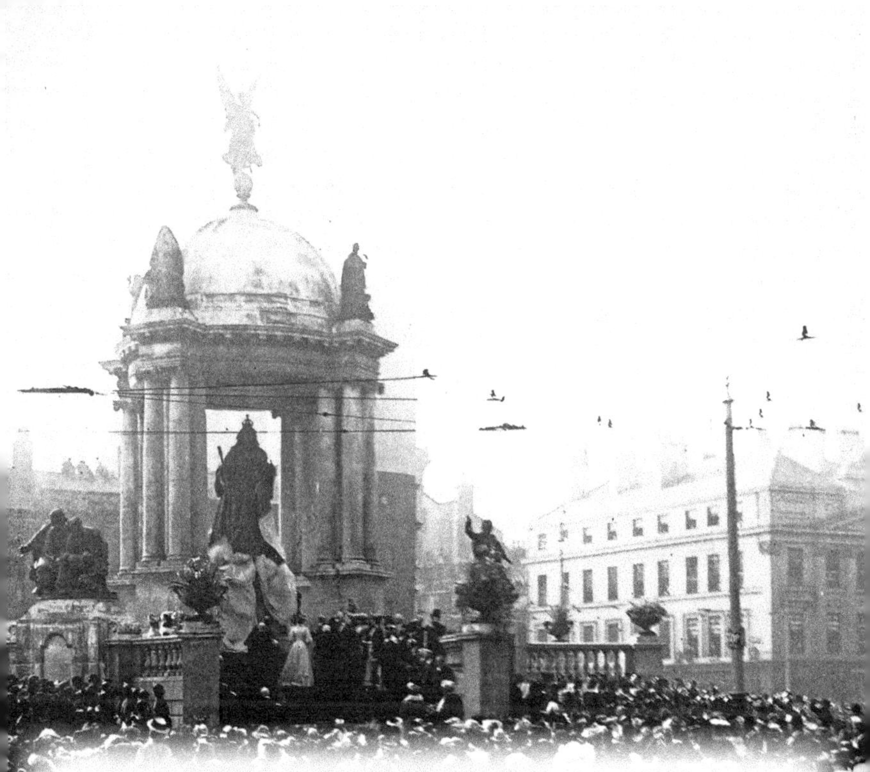

13. VICTORIA MONUMENT

The Victoria Monument was built of Portland stone in 1901 on the site of St George's Church, which was demolished in 1897. The foundation stone was laid on 11 October 1902 and it was unveiled on 27 September 1906. It is a Grade II-listed structure and was designed by F. M. Simpson, who was the first Professor of Architecture at the University of Liverpool. The four sections around the monument represent Agriculture, Commerce, Education and Industry. The Victoria Monument is made of bronze, 14 feet in height, clad in robes of state, beneath a dome and supported by four groups of four columns. The dome, surmounted by a figure of Victory, is 56 feet above the pavement.

14. BANK OF ENGLAND BUILDING

The Bank of England Building was designed by Charles Robert Cockerell and was constructed in neoclassical style between 1845 and 1848. It is situated in Castle Street, which is the heart of the business district with banks, shipping offices and insurance companies, and was built as one of three branches for the Bank of England in a combination of Greek, Roman and Renaissance styles. It was described by Nikolaus Pevsner as a 'masterpiece of Victorian architecture.'

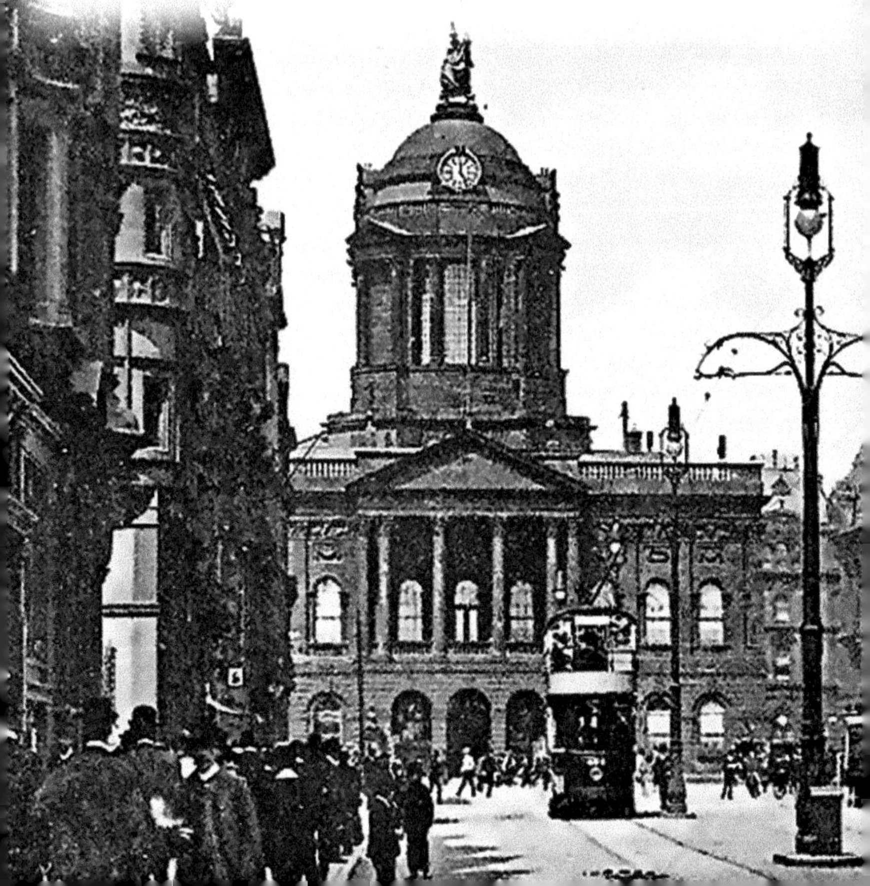

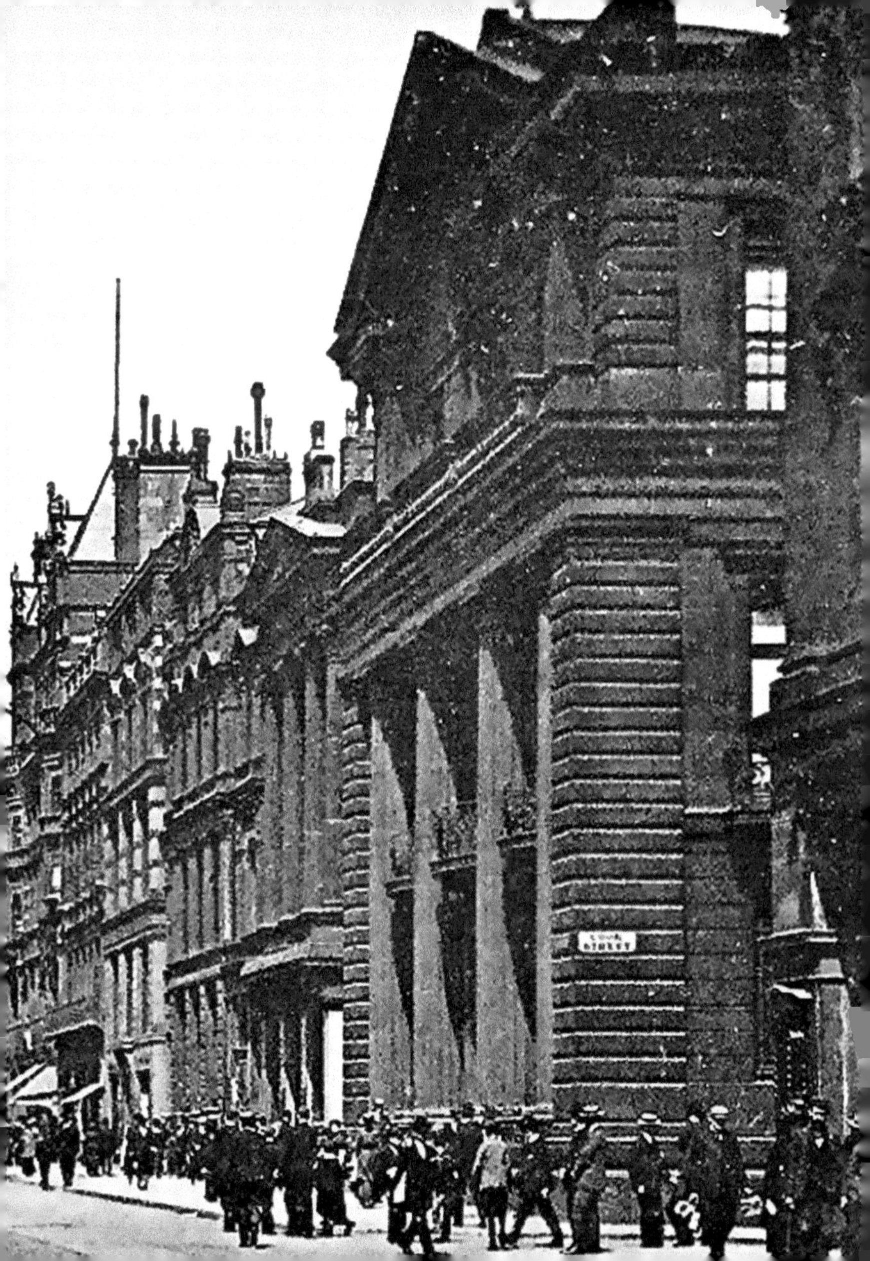

15. NATIONAL WESTMINSTER BANK

Castle Street looking toward the Victoria Monument. The building on the right is the National Westminster Bank, which was designed by Norman Shaw and completed in 1900 as Parr's Bank. The basement is of smooth grey granite with a rusticated, round arch entrance. There are bands of grey-green and cream marble, the window surrounds and the cornice is of red terracotta. The banking hall, which is lit by a shallow central dome, has offices above and is supported by steel trusses. It is in French Renaissance style, the second-floor windows are ogee headed and cusped, the third floor are narrow and round headed, and the fourth floor are round arched. Tall stone chimneys rise from the roof.

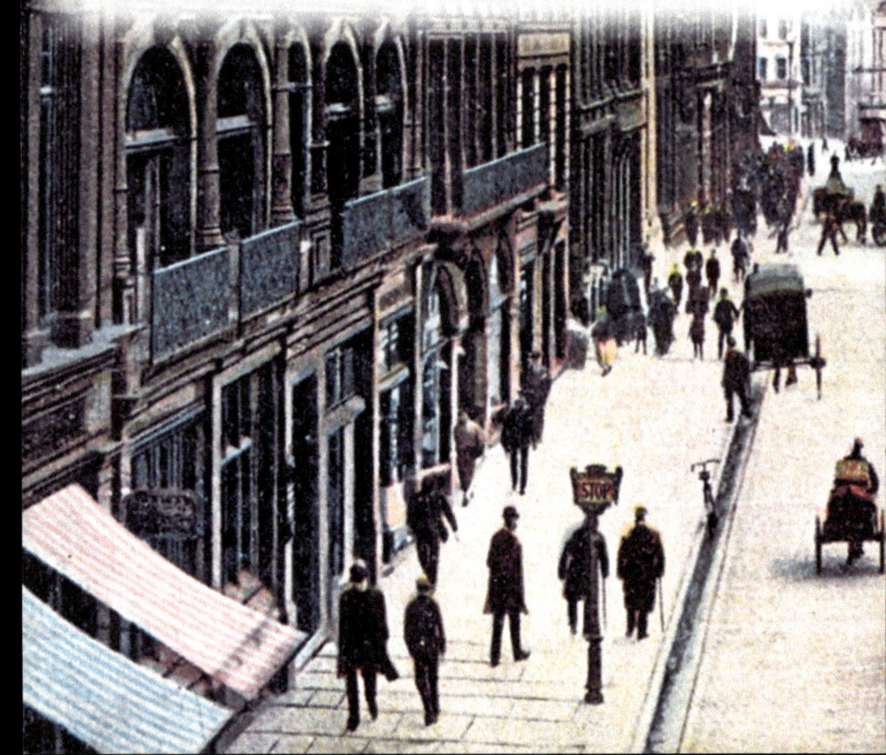

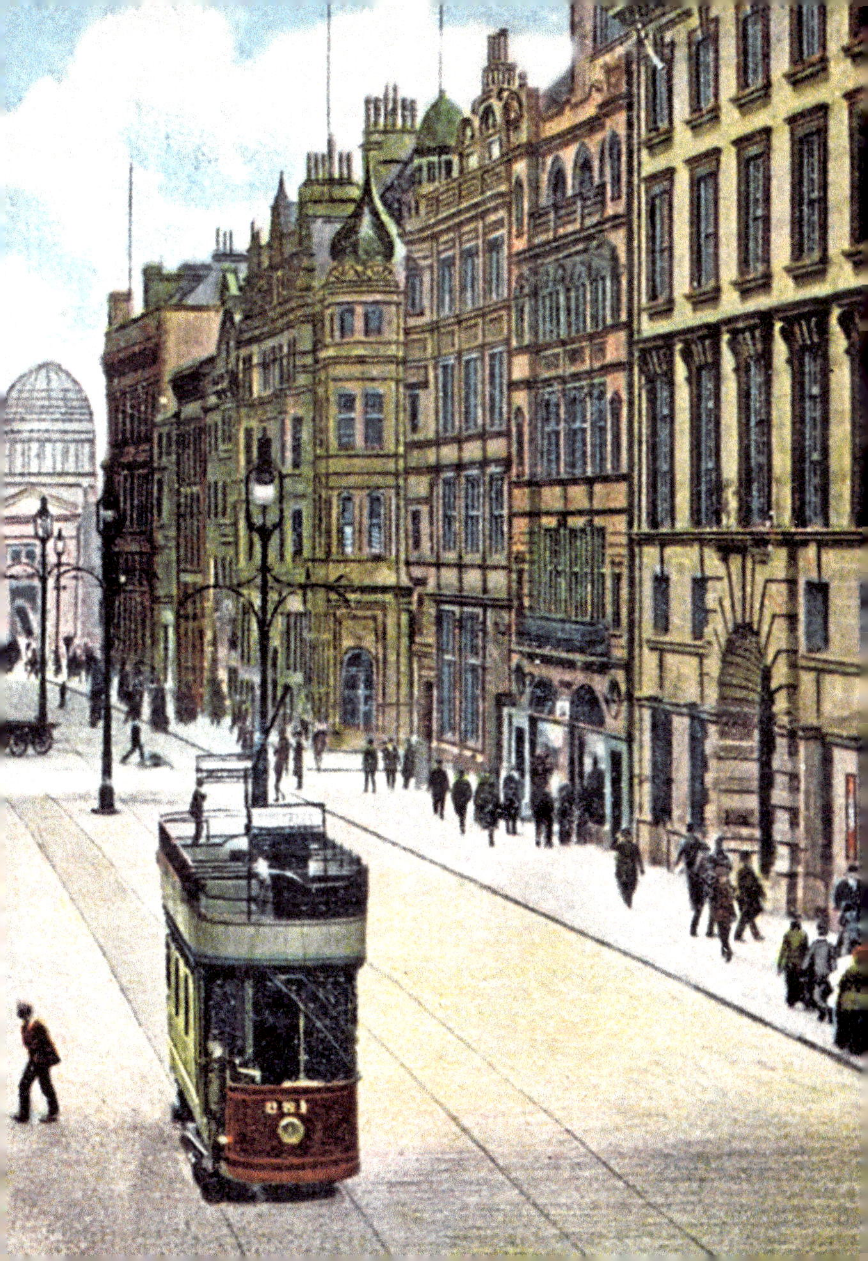

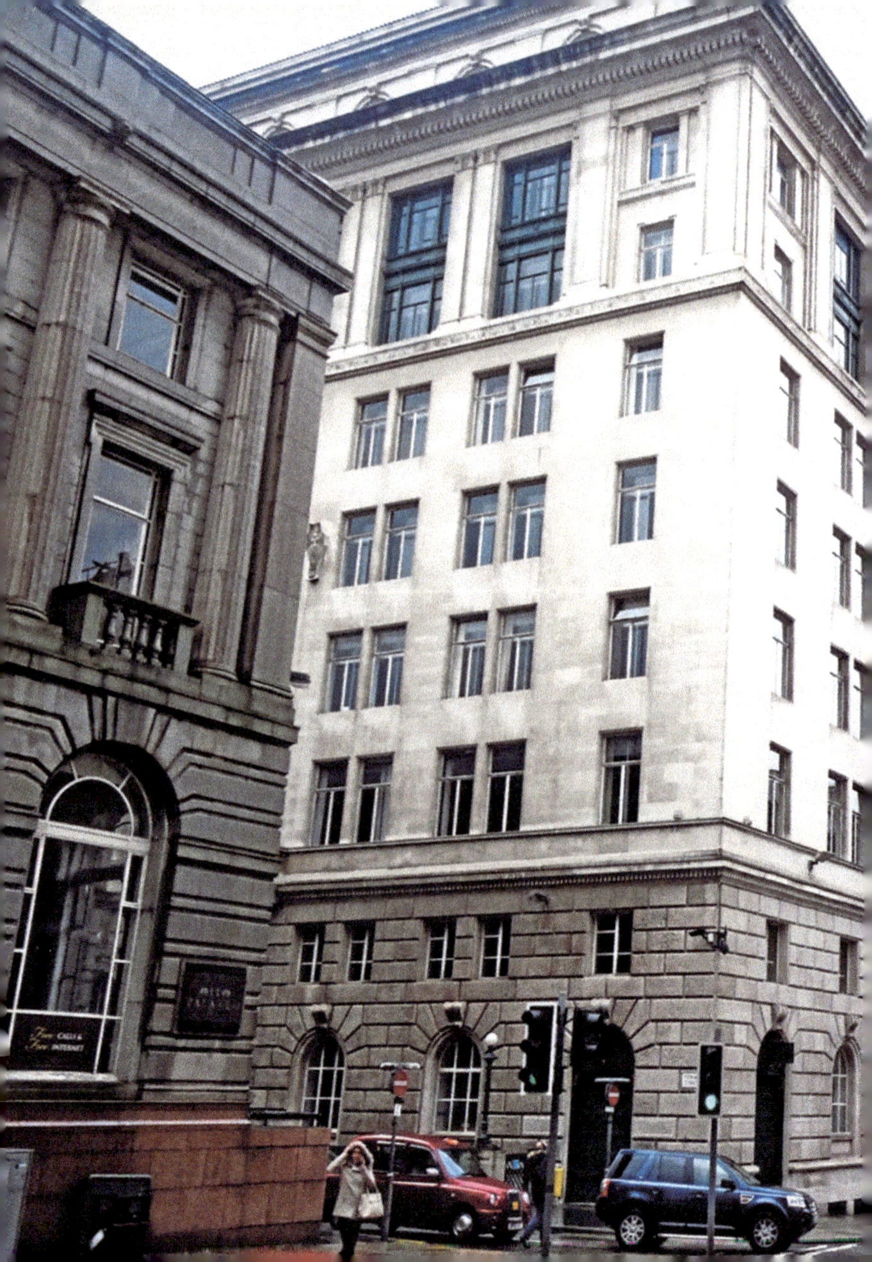

16. INDIA BUILDINGS

India Building was designed by Arnold Thornely and Herbert J. Rowse, and was built between 1924 and 1932. It was financed by Alfred Holt & Co. Ltd for its own use and to let office space to other businesses. The building was constructed by Dove Brothers of Islington, with steelwork from Dorman Long of Middlesbrough, and cost £1.25 million. It replaced an older India Building on the site, which was built in 1830 for George Holt. The second India Building was built in two stages, with the first constructed alongside the earlier building, and the second stage demolishing and replacing the original. At the planning approval stage it was decided to incorporate an arcade of shops, which would run from the front of the building to the back.

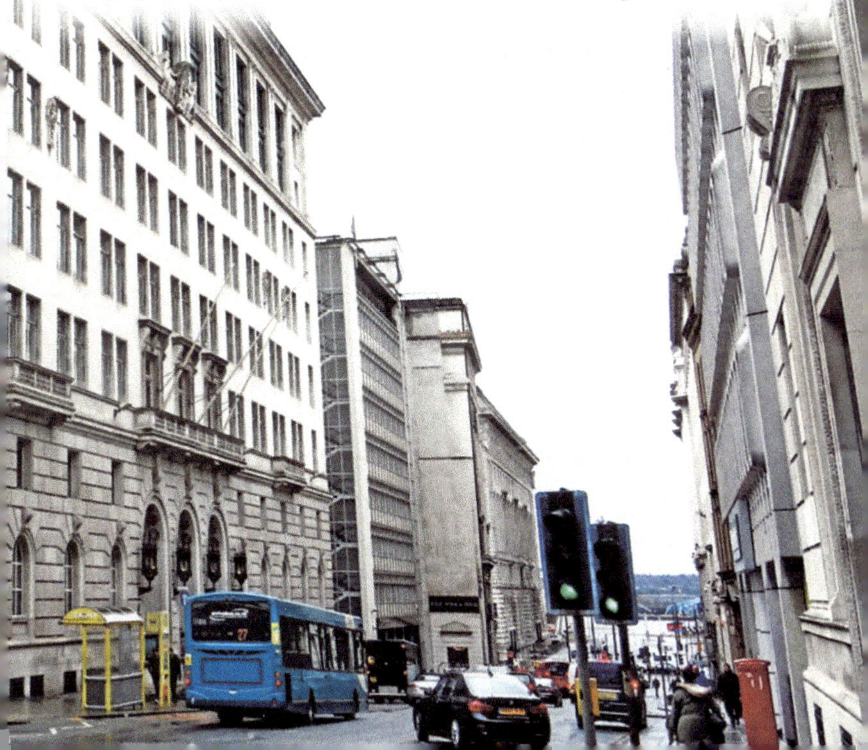

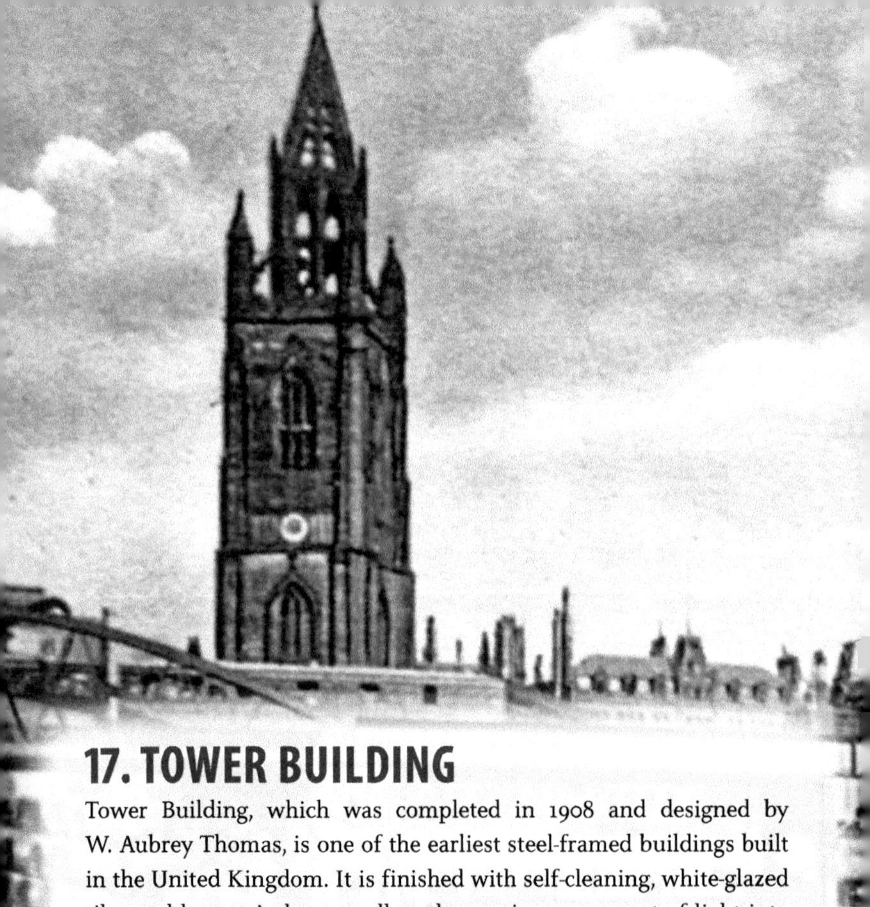

17. TOWER BUILDING

Tower Building, which was completed in 1908 and designed by W. Aubrey Thomas, is one of the earliest steel-framed buildings built in the United Kingdom. It is finished with self-cleaning, white-glazed tiles and large windows to allow the maximum amount of light into the building. Sir John Stanley built the first Tower in 1406; during the eighteenth century the Tower of Liverpool, between Tower Gardens and Stringers Alley, was the main jail of Liverpool. The Tower was demolished in 1819 and replaced by warehouses, and by 1856 a second Tower Building containing offices was built on the site. This building was demolished only fifty years later. The present building was opened in 1910.

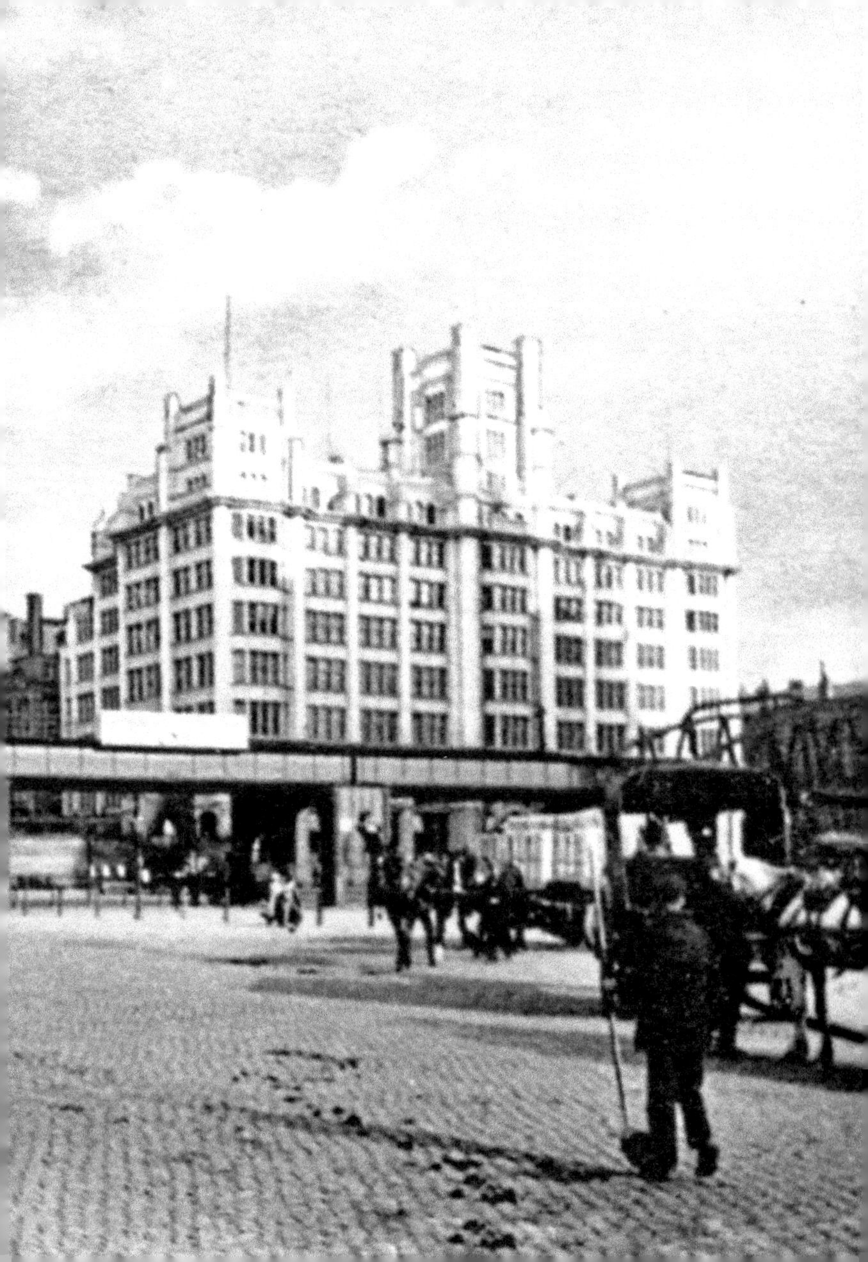

18. CHURCH OF OUR LADY AND ST NICHOLAS

Georges Dock was opened in 1771. The dock, together with the adjoining George's Basin, was filled in creating the Pier Head. The Church of Our Lady and St Nicholas is frequently referred to as the sailor's church. St Mary del Quay was a small place of worship that was built on the site in the mid-thirteenth century until a new chapel was built nearly 100 years later. This was dedicated to St Mary and St Nicholas and when a plague hit the town in 1361, it was licensed as a burial ground. The chapel was extended in the fifteenth century and by 1515 the church contained four chantry alters. At the beginning of the eighteenth century, when Liverpool became an independent parish, St Nicholas and St Peter's became the parish churches. The church was extended again in 1775.

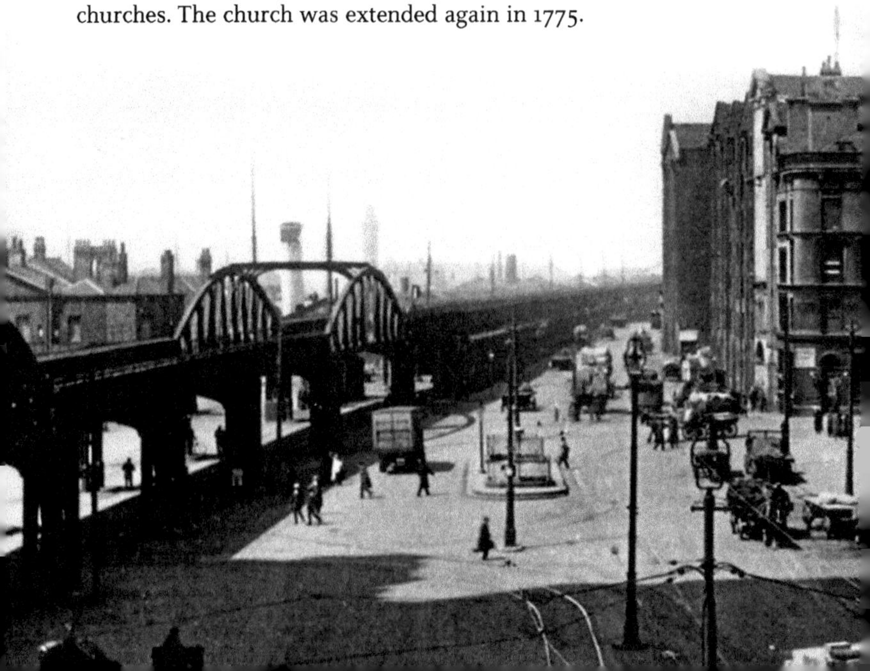

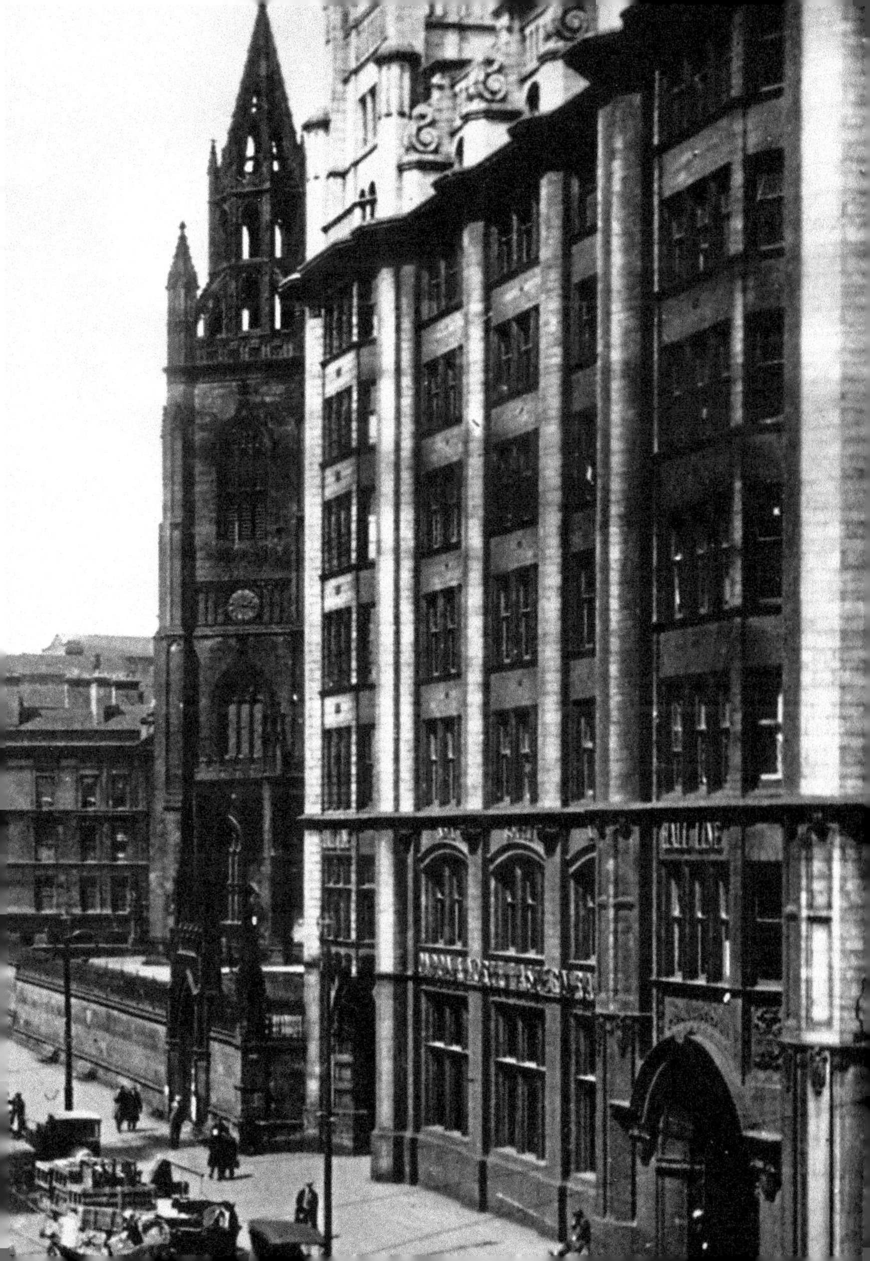

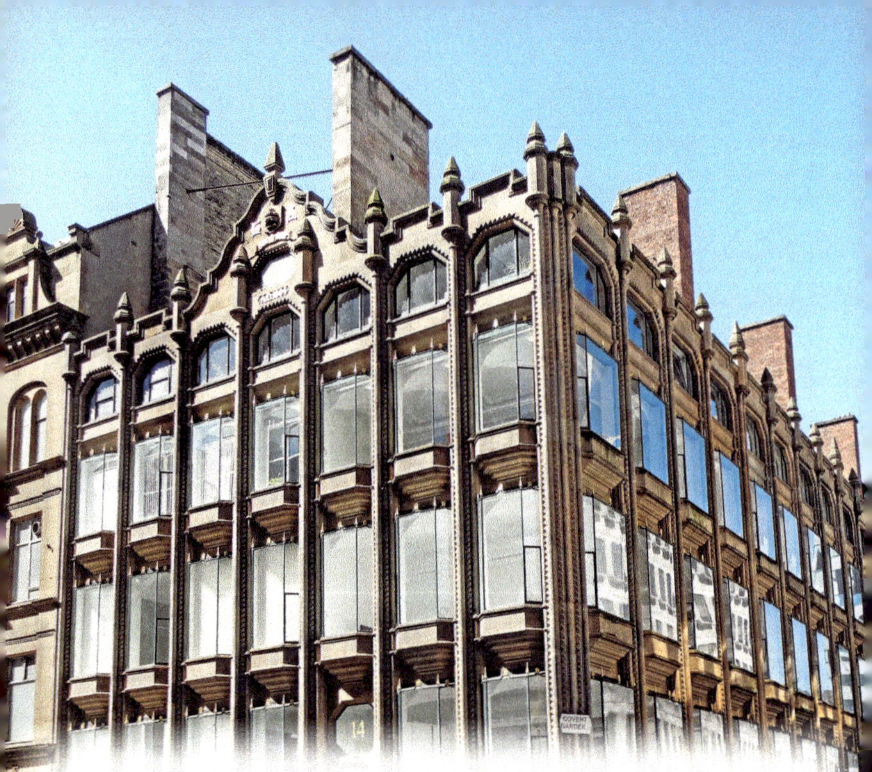

19. ORIEL CHAMBERS

Oriel Chambers, together with the Jayne Building in Philadelphia, was one of the world's first buildings that featured a metal-framed glass curtain wall. The building comprises 43,000 square feet of floor space over five storeys. It was designed by Peter Ellis, who used light by employing a grid of oriel windows and many of the techniques he used were later incorporated into skyscrapers built in America in the 1880s. Nikolaus Pevsner called it, 'one of the most remarkable buildings of its date in Europe' and 'The delicacy of the ironwork in the plate-glass oriel windows and the curtain walling at the back with the vertical supports retracted yet visible from outside is almost unbelievably ahead of its time.'

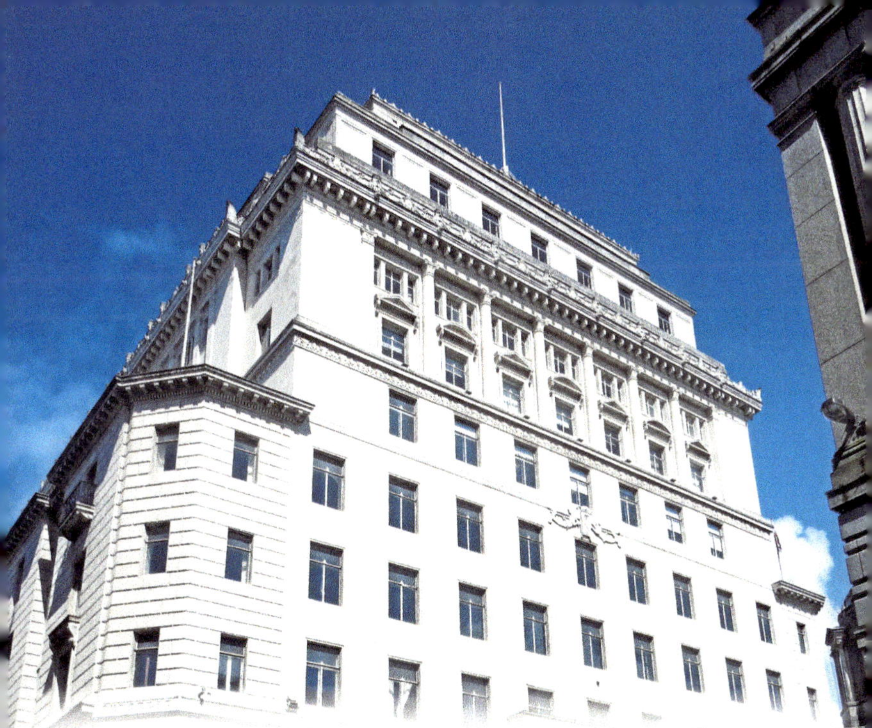

20. MARTINS BANK HEAD OFFICE

The Liverpool head office of Martins Bank was opened for business on 24 October 1932 and is a Grade II-listed building, designed by Herbert Rowse. Martins Bank was acquired by the Bank of Liverpool in 1918 and it was renamed the Bank of Liverpool & Martins Bank. The name was shortened in 1928 to Martins Bank Limited with 560 branches. Martins Bank Building was constructed between 1927 and 1932 and has a steel frame with Portland stone. It is ten storeys high, with the upper ones set back. The central entrance leads to a banking hall with island counters and vaulted arcades on four sides. The exterior walls were washed down in the 1970s, which dramatically improved the appearance of the building; Martins Bank Building was sold in 2003 with a temporary lease-back of the banking hall.

21. LIVERPOOL TOWN HALL

Liverpool Town Hall in Castle Street is the city's third and was designed by John Wood of Bath and is designated as a Grade I-listed building. The first town hall was replaced in 1673 by a building just south of the present building, which stood on pillars and arches of stone. The present town hall was built between 1749 and 1754; an extension to the north, designed by James Wyatt, was added in 1785. A serious fire severely damaged the hall in 1795 and it was rebuilt with a dome added and the work was completed in 1802. A central courtyard was replaced with a hall containing a staircase, a portico was added to the south side, and the work, including the decoration, was completed by 1820. The building was damaged by bombing and air raids during the Second World War. A restoration programme of work was completed in 1995.

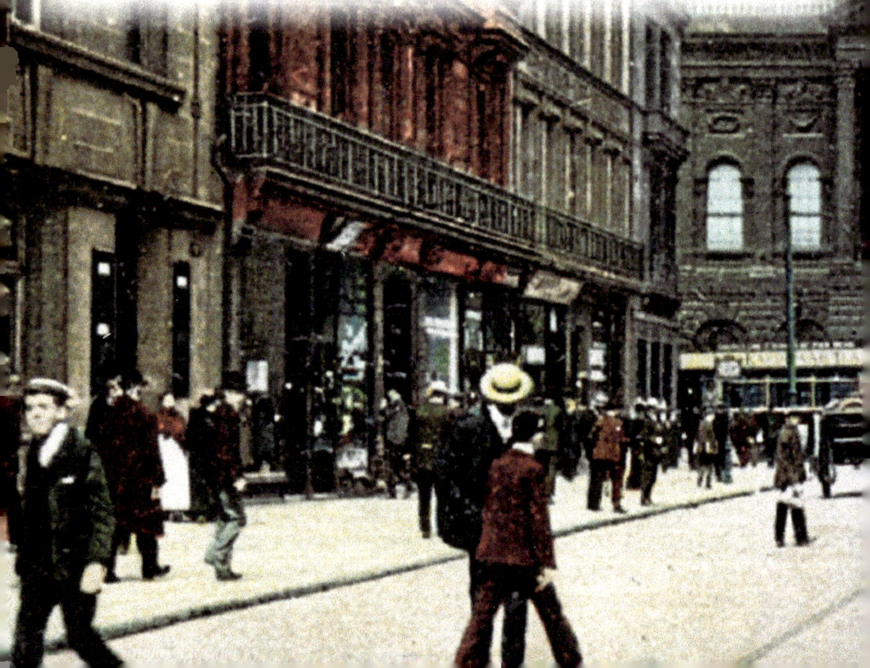

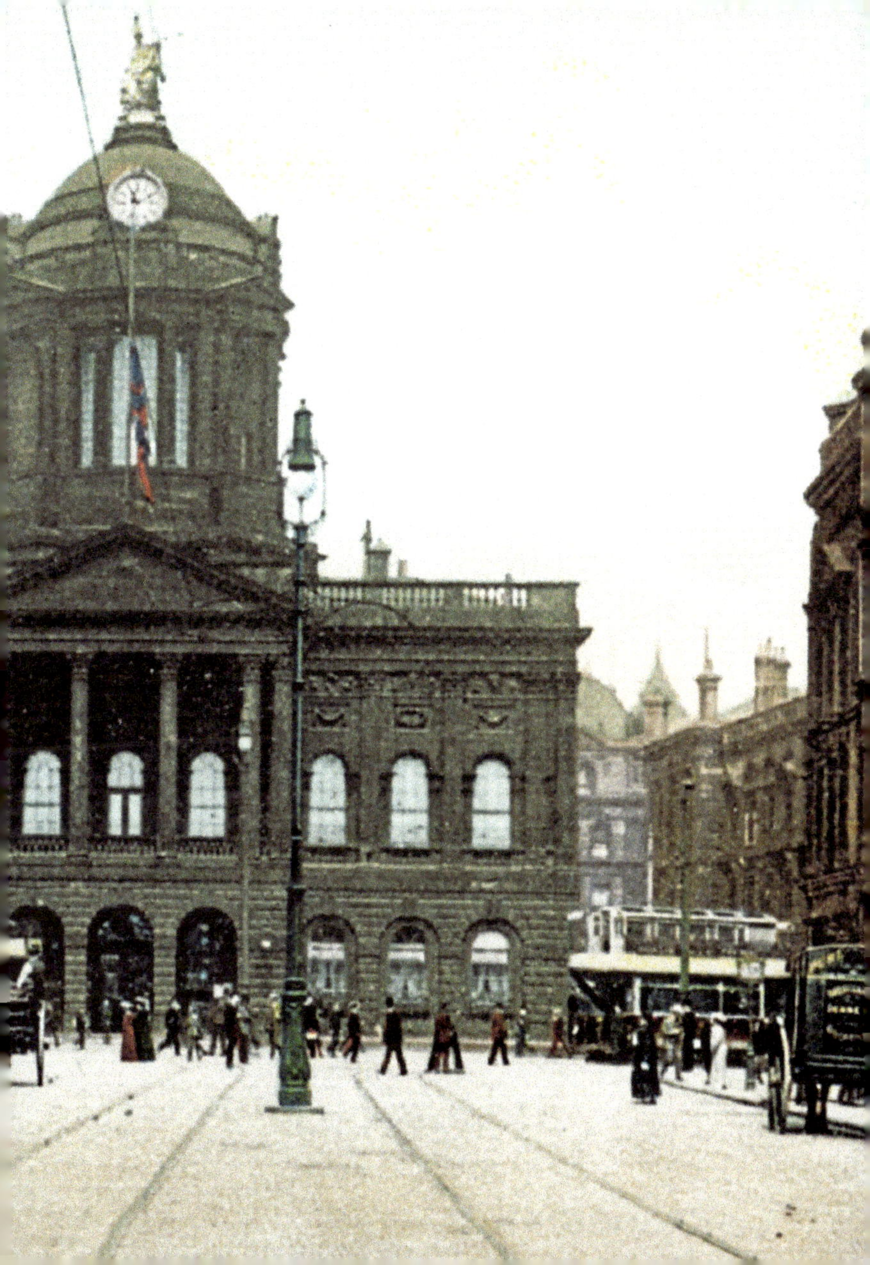

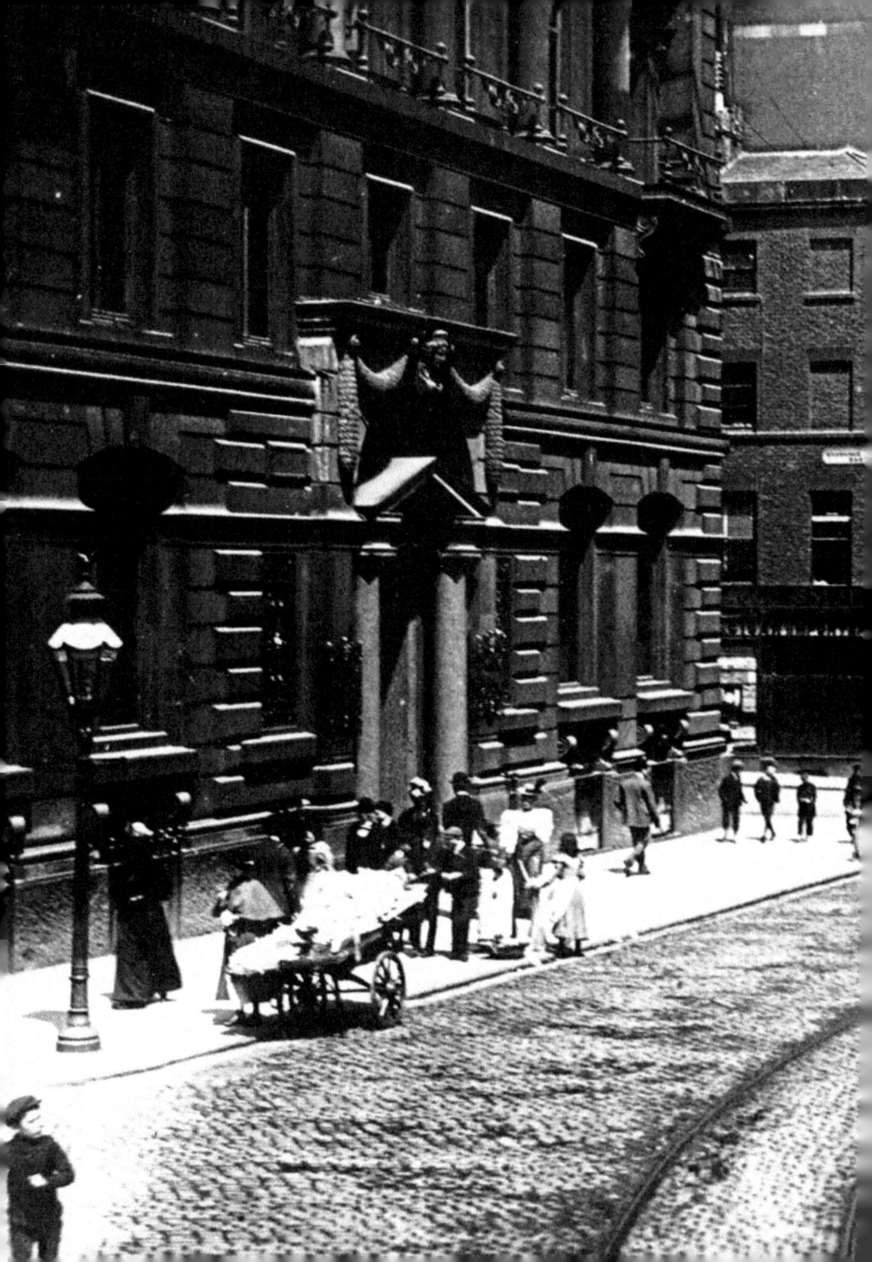

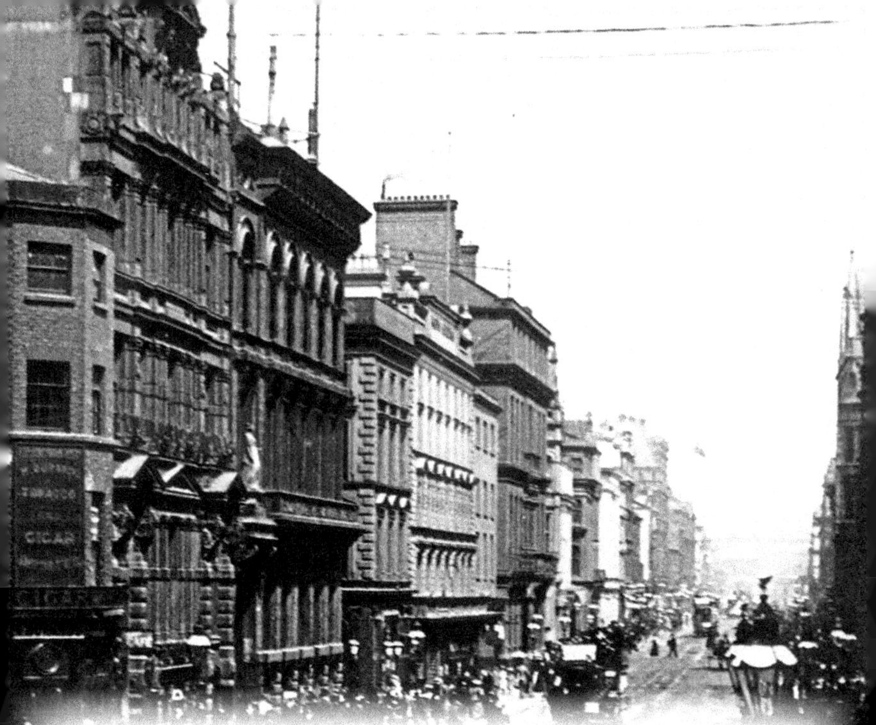

22. LIVERPOOL, LONDON AND GLOBE BUILDING

A view looking up Dale Street from the northern end of Castle Street. The building on the left was built as the Liverpool and London & Globe Insurance Co. between 1855 and 1857, designed by C. R. Cockerell, his son F. P. Cockerell and Christopher F. Heyward. The building is constructed in ashlar, with rusticated quoins and a slate roof. It is three storeys high with a basement and attics. On Dale Street there are seven bays, and fifteen bays along the sides. The Queen Insurance Building is opposite and was designed by Samuel Rowland for the Royal Bank and was completed in 1839.

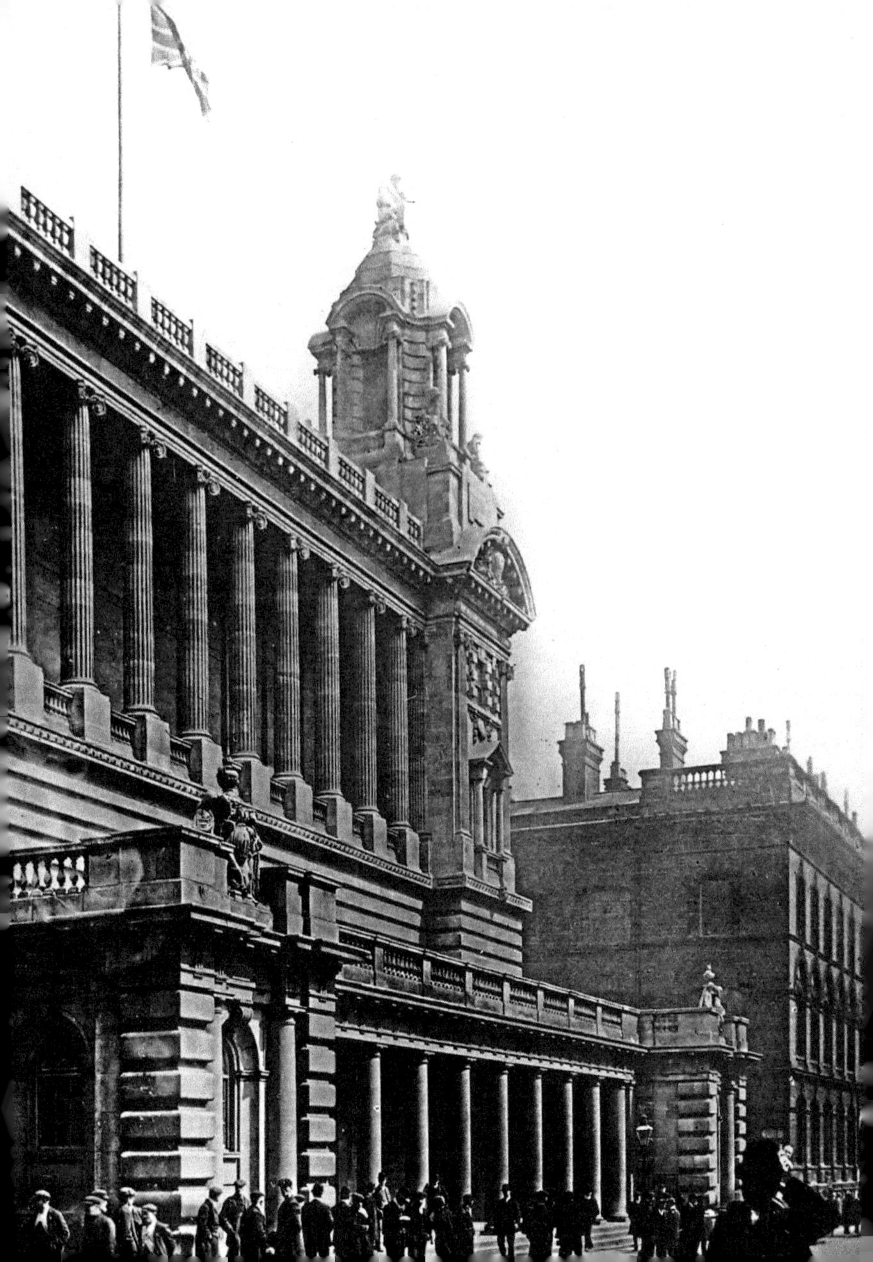

23. COTTON EXCHANGE

The Cotton Exchange in Old Hall Street was built in 1905–06 and originally had a neoclassical façade with Portland stone columns and twin baroque towers. These were demolished in 1967 but the polished grey columns of Norwegian granite still survive, as do the original side and rear elevations. The sculpture in Old Hall Street represents the River Mersey, and two in the courtyard represent Navigation and Commerce. The first American cotton to be shipped to Liverpool arrived at the port in 1784. Cotton was imported from Brazil, Egypt and India and by 1850 cotton accounted for almost half the city's trade. Initially the cotton merchants met on Exchange flags to sell and buy the commodity; an Exchange was opened in 1808 but the merchants continued to deal in the square until the end of the nineteenth century.

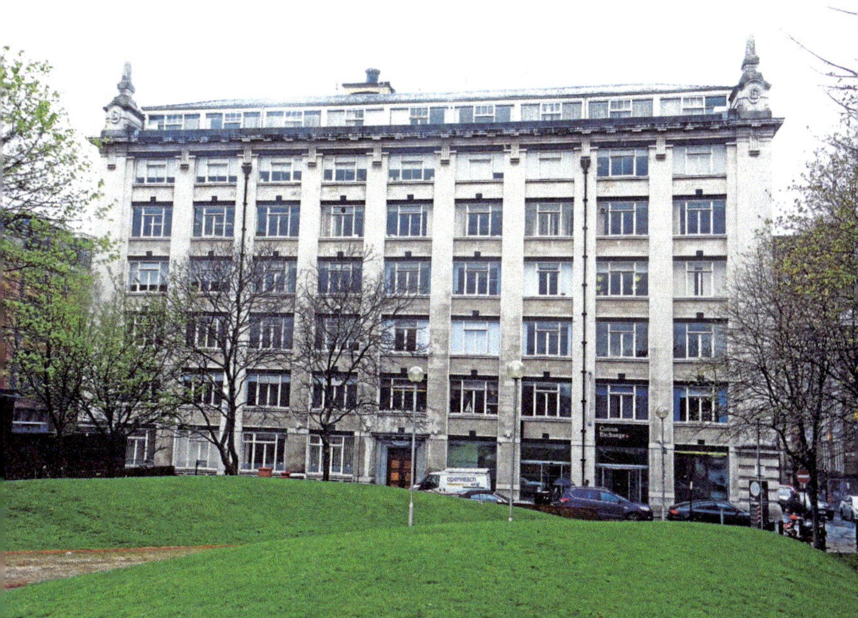

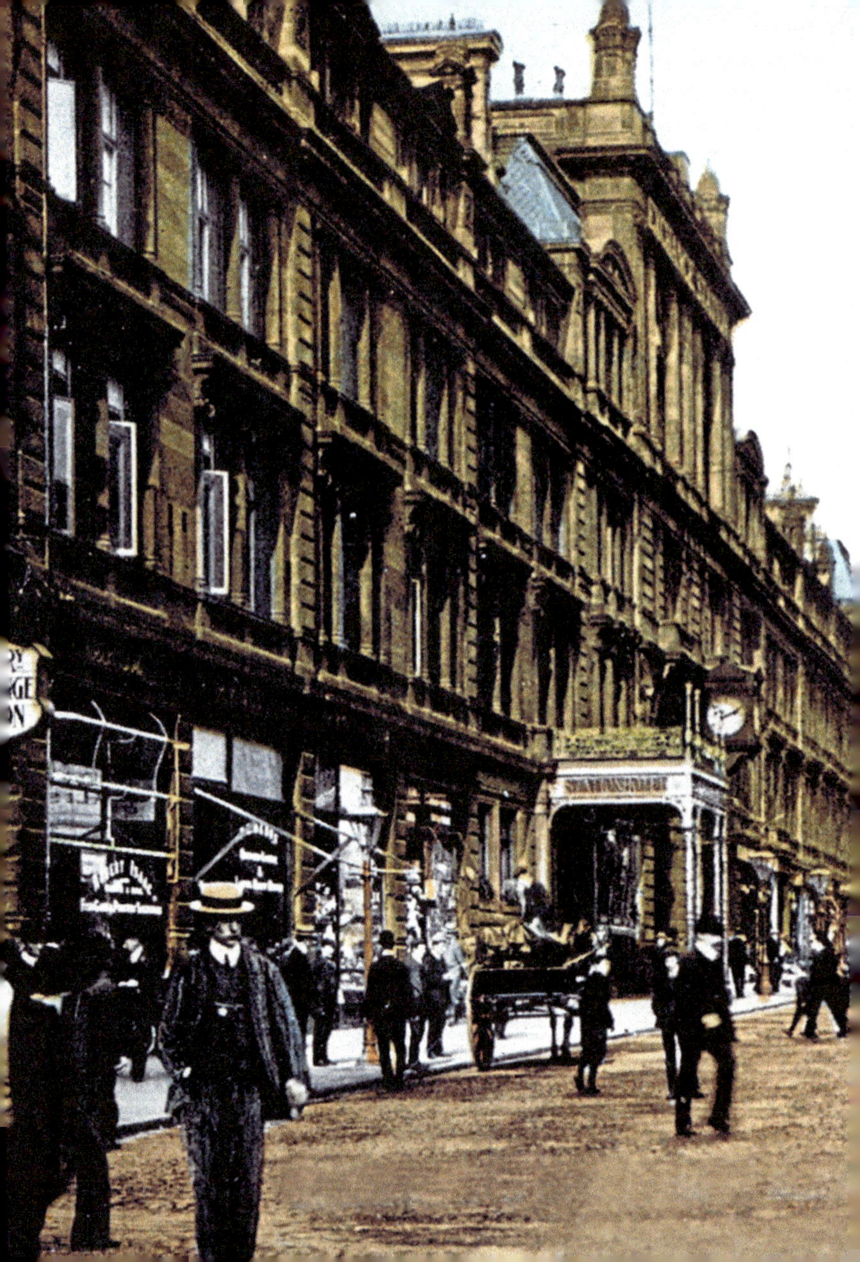

24. LIVERPOOL EXCHANGE STATION

Exchange Station was opened on 13 May 1850 and originally had two names. The Lancashire & Yorkshire Railway named it Liverpool Exchange Station, and the East Lancashire Railway named it Liverpool Tithebarn Street. It became Liverpool Exchange on 13 August 1859. From 1 October 1850 trains of the Liverpool, Crosby & Southport Railway used it as a terminus. As it became inadequate to deal with the traffic, it was rebuilt between 1886 and 1888, and had a grand reopening on 2 July 1888. The station was the terminus of the Lancashire & Yorkshire Railway, providing services to Manchester Victoria, Blackpool North and the Lake District, Whitehaven and Glasgow Central. The main station was closed on the 30 April 1977 and Moorfields Station opened the following week to provide services by Merseyrail.

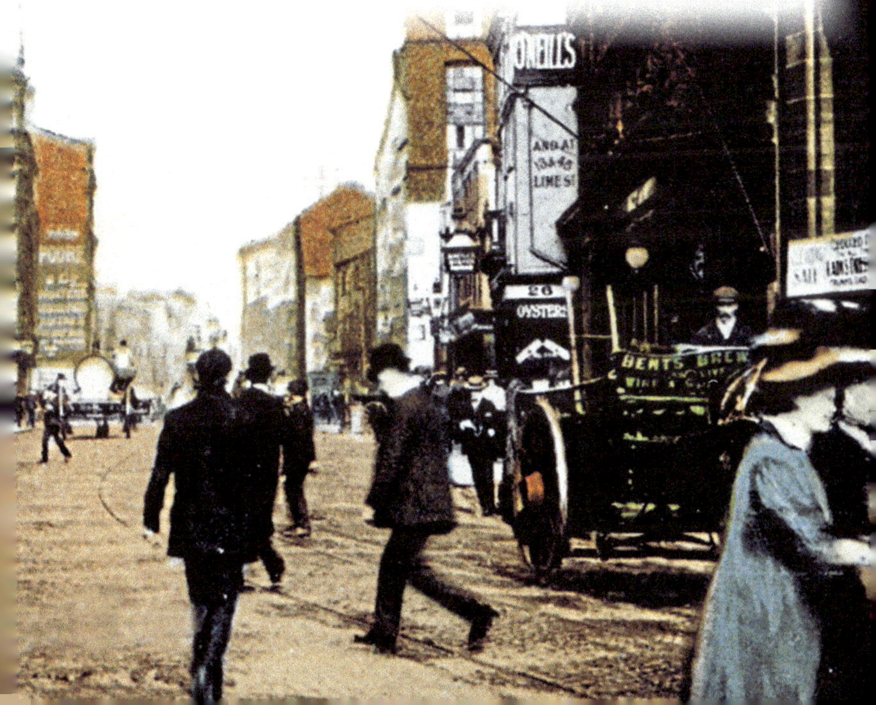

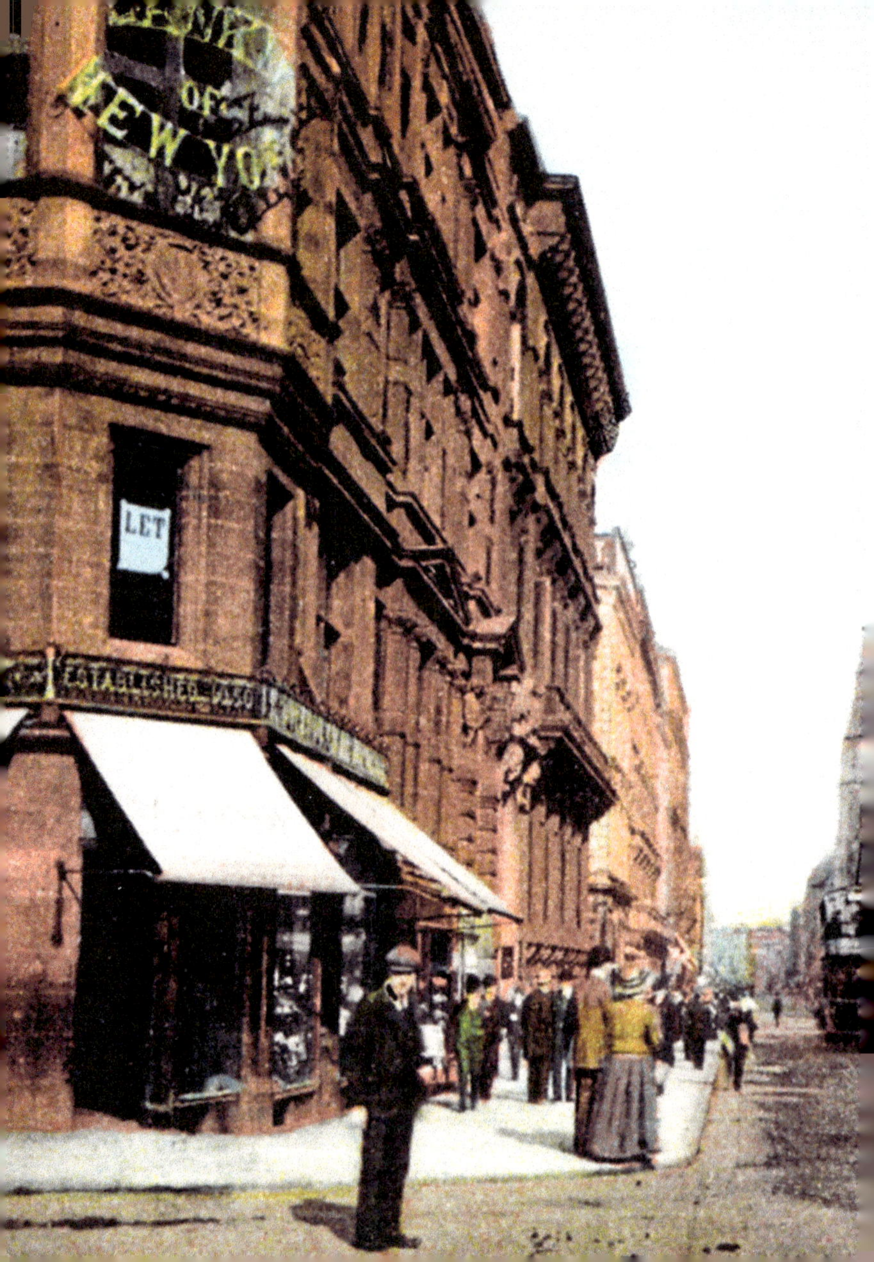
OF
NEW YOR
LET

25. ROYAL INSURANCE BUILDING

The building with the dome in the centre of the picture is the Royal Insurance Building, which is on the corner of Dale Street and North John Street. It was built between 1897 and 1903 and was designed by J. Francis Doyle after a competition short list of seven designs. Norman Shaw was retained as the 'advisory architect' as Doyle had worked with Shaw on the White Star Building in James Street. It is built in granite and Portland stone over a steel frame. There is a long façade to North John Street, with an off-centre entrance under a gold domed tower.

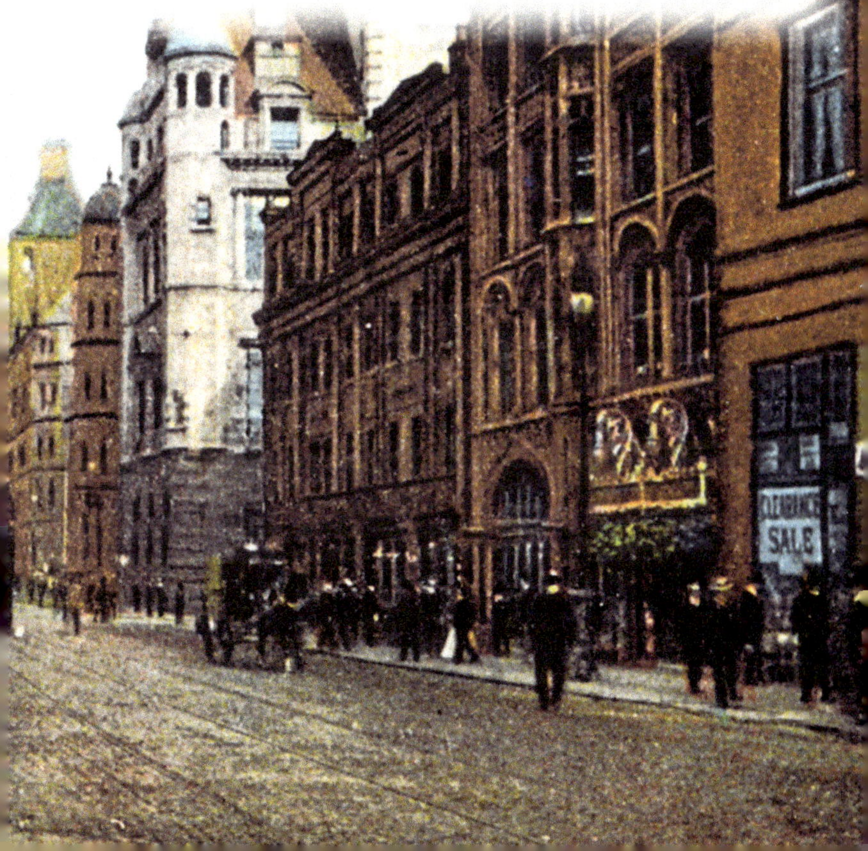

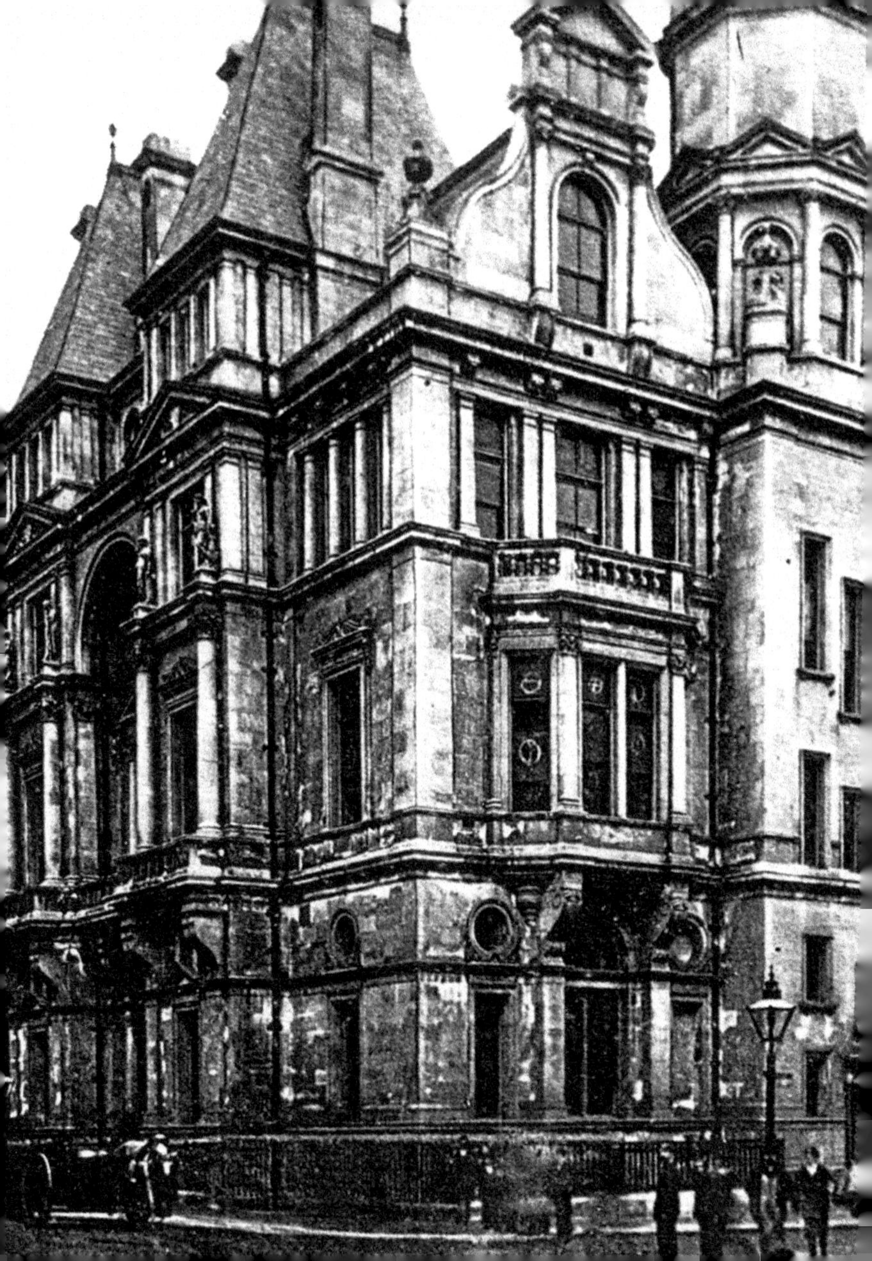

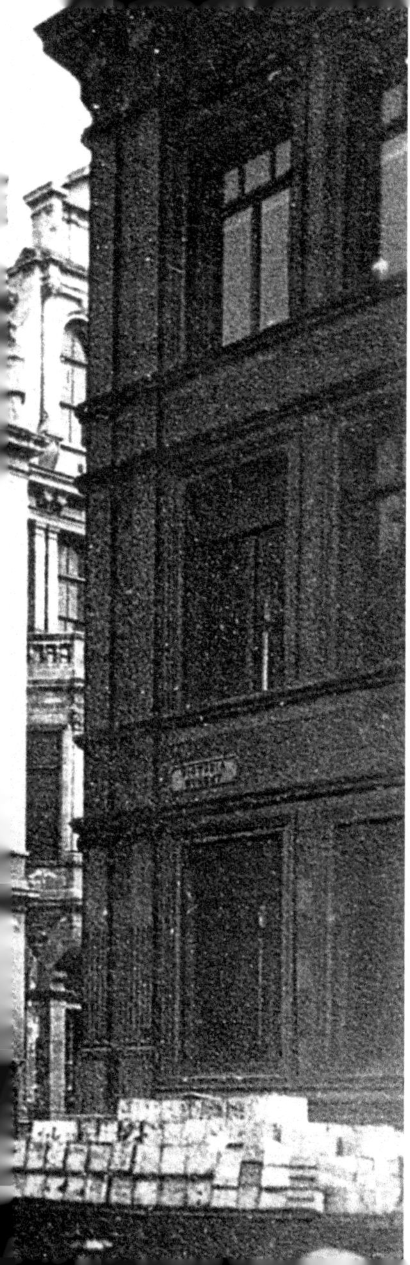

26. GENERAL POST OFFICE

The General Post Office in Victoria Street was constructed between 1894 and 1899 and was designed by Henry Tanner. The building resembled a Loire chateau with a skyline of shaped gables, chimneys and pavilion roofs. The decoration included sculpture by Edward O. Griffith around the main entrance. The Ward Lock Guide to Liverpool describes the Post Office: 'With the exception of St Martin's-le-Grande, London, the Liverpool Post Office is perhaps the largest and most important in the kingdom.' The building was owned by the Walton Group and was acquired by Milligan and J. W. Kaempfer and Richardson Developments in 2004 and converted into a 160,000-square-foot shopping centre named the Metquarter.

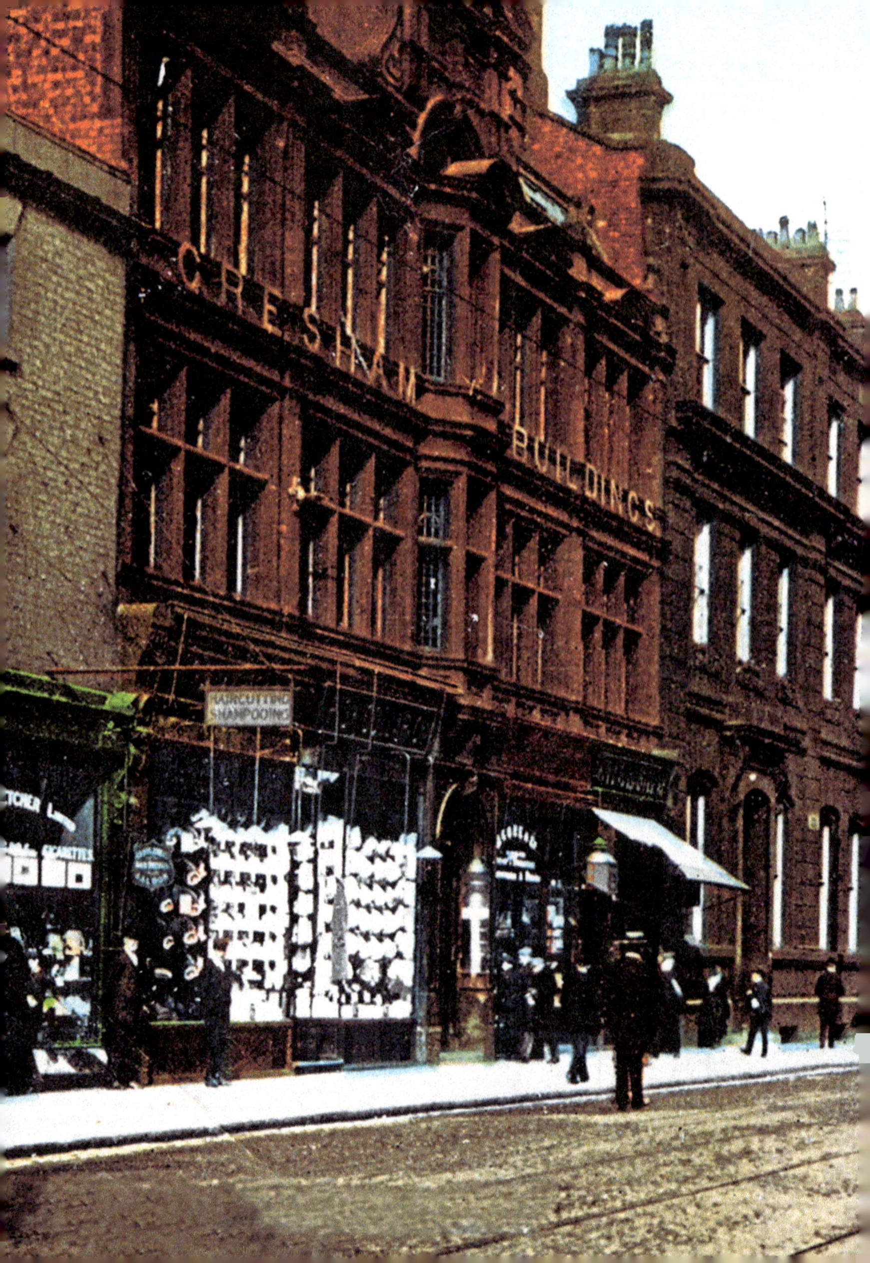
GRESHAM
BUILDINGS
HAIRCUTTING
SHAMPOOING

27. MAGISTRATES' COURT

The magistrates' court at the top of Dale Street was built in 1857–59 and designed by John Weightman. The juvenile courts are in the same complex but are accessible from around the corner in Hatton Garden. It is a three-storey ashlar building with a central pediment and carriage entrance below. The Main Bridewell, also designed by Weightman, is behind the magistrates' court and is accessible from Cheapside. It is a neoclassical prison building, with the front being separated by a courtyard with gates at the entrance. The magistrates' court is a Grade II-listed building and it was announced in 2007 that they would close and be replaced by new purpose-built facilities. On 23 June 2015, more than 150 years of justice was marked when the magistrates' court closed and moved to the Queen Elizabeth II Law Courts in Derby Square.

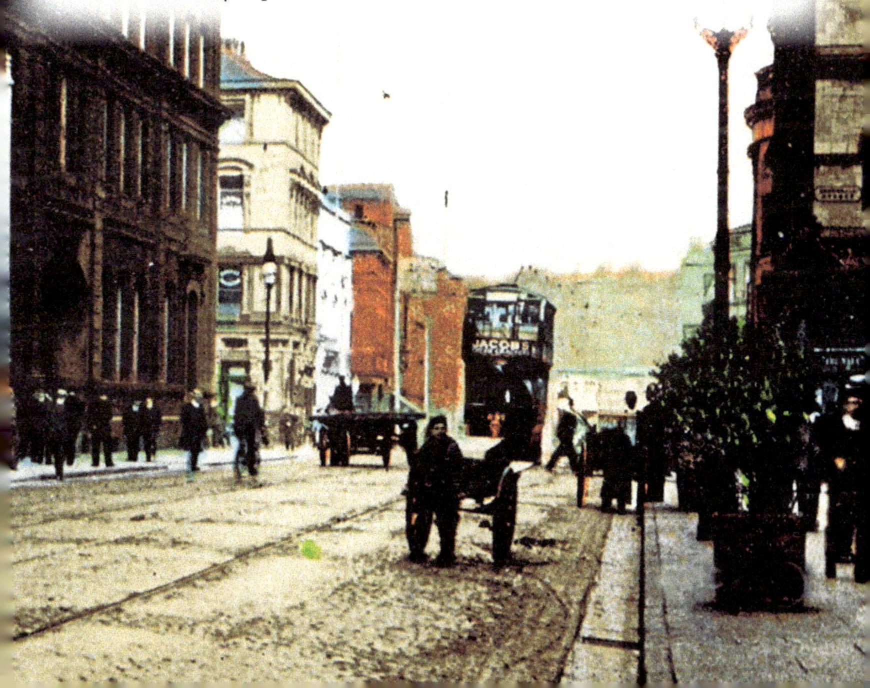

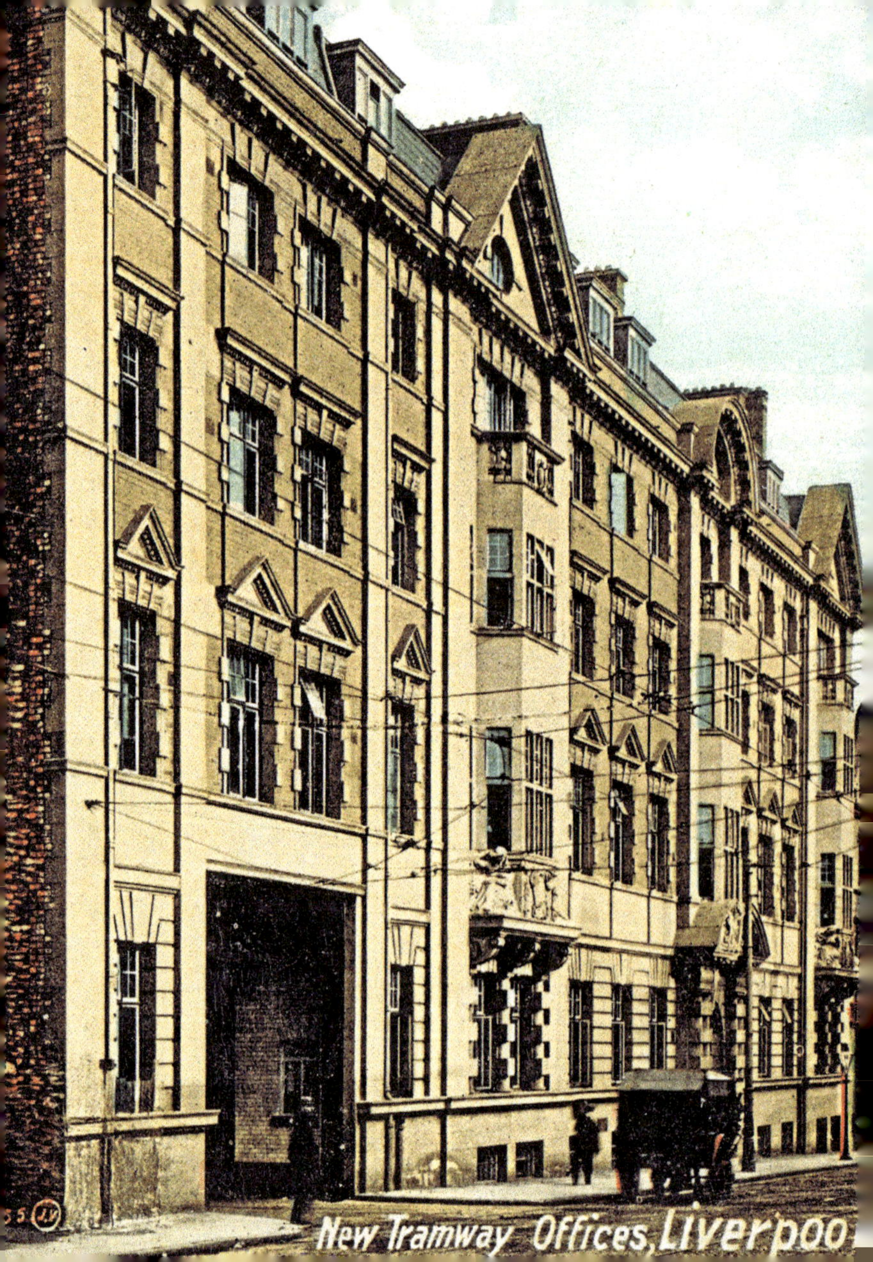
New Tramway Offices, Liverpoo

28. THE TRAMWAYS BUILDING

At the beginning of the twentieth century it was intended to build the head office for the trams on reclaimed land at Georges Dock. However, Hatton Garden was purchased near the central police station, the central fire station and the Fire Salvage Association. The site was originally owned by John Gordon Houghton and was bought by the Corporation on 20 July 1904. The foundation stone for No. 24 Hatton Garden was laid on 12 September 1905 by the Chairman of the Tramways Committee, Sir Charles Petrie, and the building was completed in January 1907 at a cost of £48,650. On the 30 June 1985 the building was given Grade II-listed-building status, then on 26 October 1986 public transport was deregulated and it became the headquarters for the Merseyside Passenger Transport Executive.

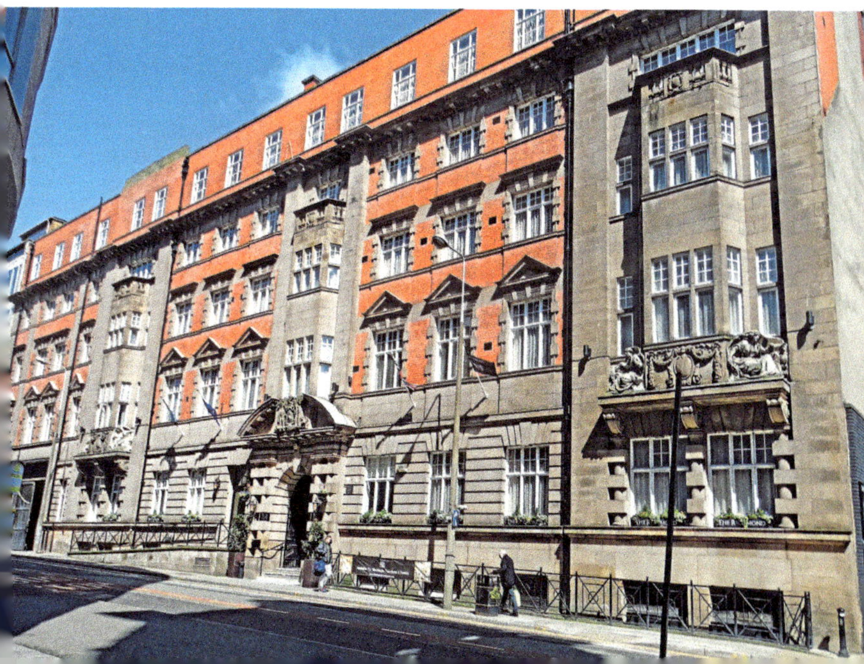

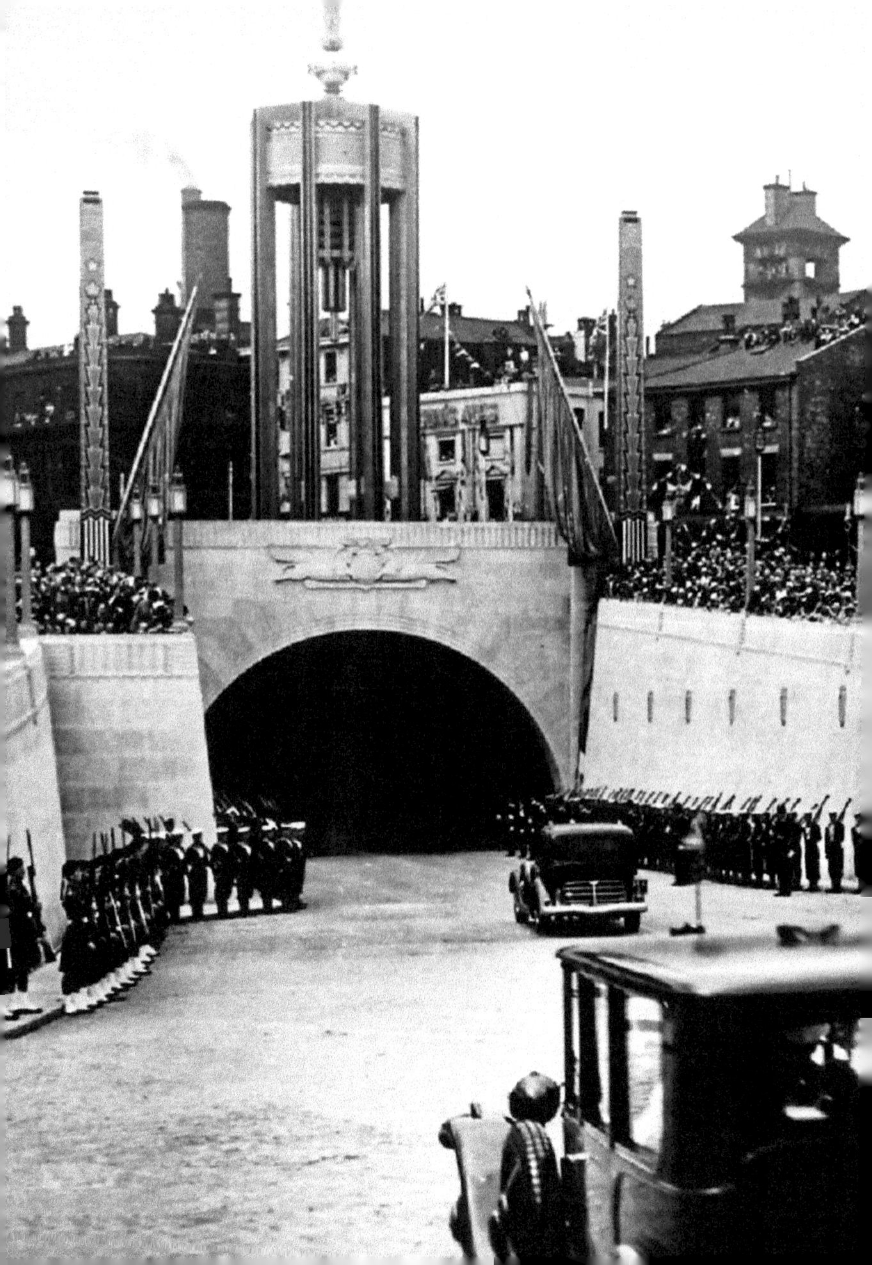

29. THE MERSEY TUNNEL

A tunnel under the River Mersey was first proposed in 1825 and there are reports that the Benedictine monks at Birkenhead Priory had earlier found a way of crossing to Liverpool under the river. However, by the 1920s the volume of traffic on the Mersey ferries had increased dramatically and parliamentary consent was given for the construction of a tunnel between Birkenhead and Liverpool. Sir Basil Mott was the consulting engineer and he supervised the work in association with John Brodie, city engineer of Liverpool Council. The Queensway Tunnel entrance in Liverpool was opened by George V and Queen Mary on the 18 July 1934. The tunnel is just over 2 miles long and has two dock branches leading to the dock system on either side of the Mersey.

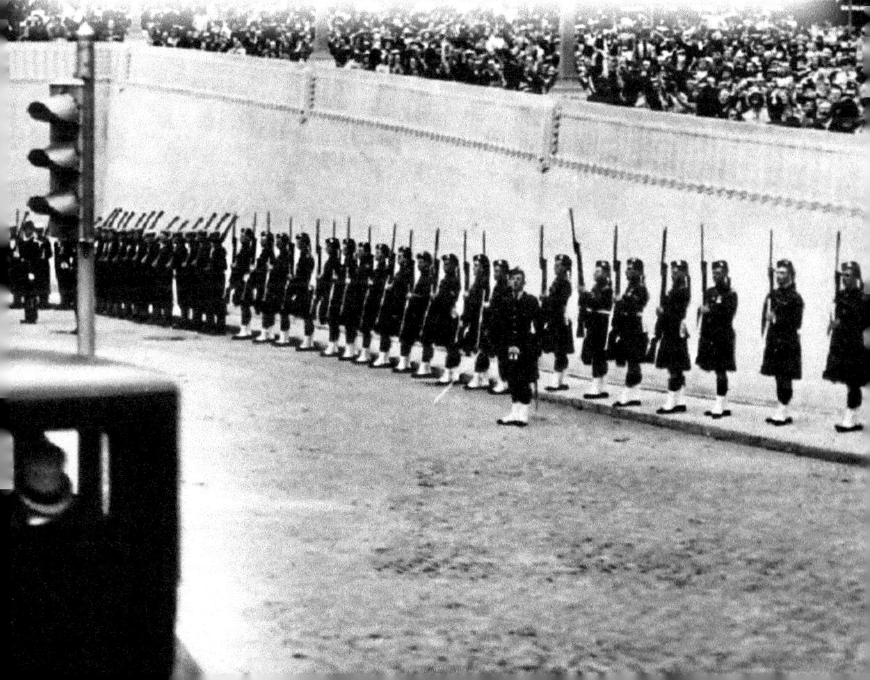

30. WILLIAM BROWN LIBRARY AND MUSEUM

A view in William Brown Street with the College of Technology and Museum Extension, which was designed by E. W. Mountford in Edwardian imperial style with sculpture by F. W. Pomeroy. The William Brown Library and Museum was designed by Thomas Allom and opened in 1860, with 400,000 people attending the opening ceremony. It is a Grade II-listed building and was designed in Corinthian style as a replacement for the Derby Museum, which contained the Earl of Derby's natural history collection. The Picton Library, Hornby Library and Oak Room were added later. It is built on Shaw's Brow and the funding was provided by Sir William Brown, First Baronet of Astrop.

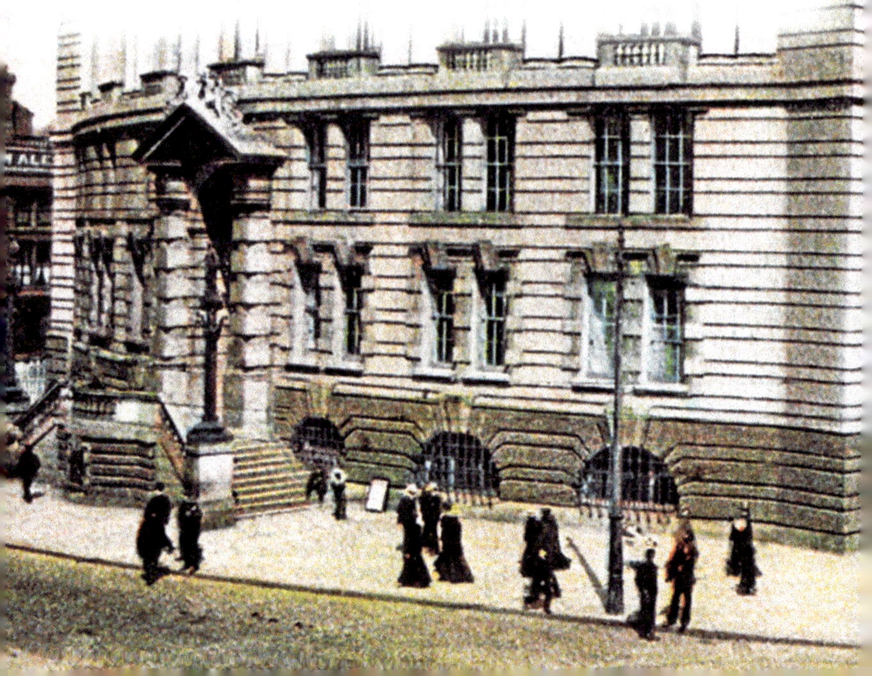

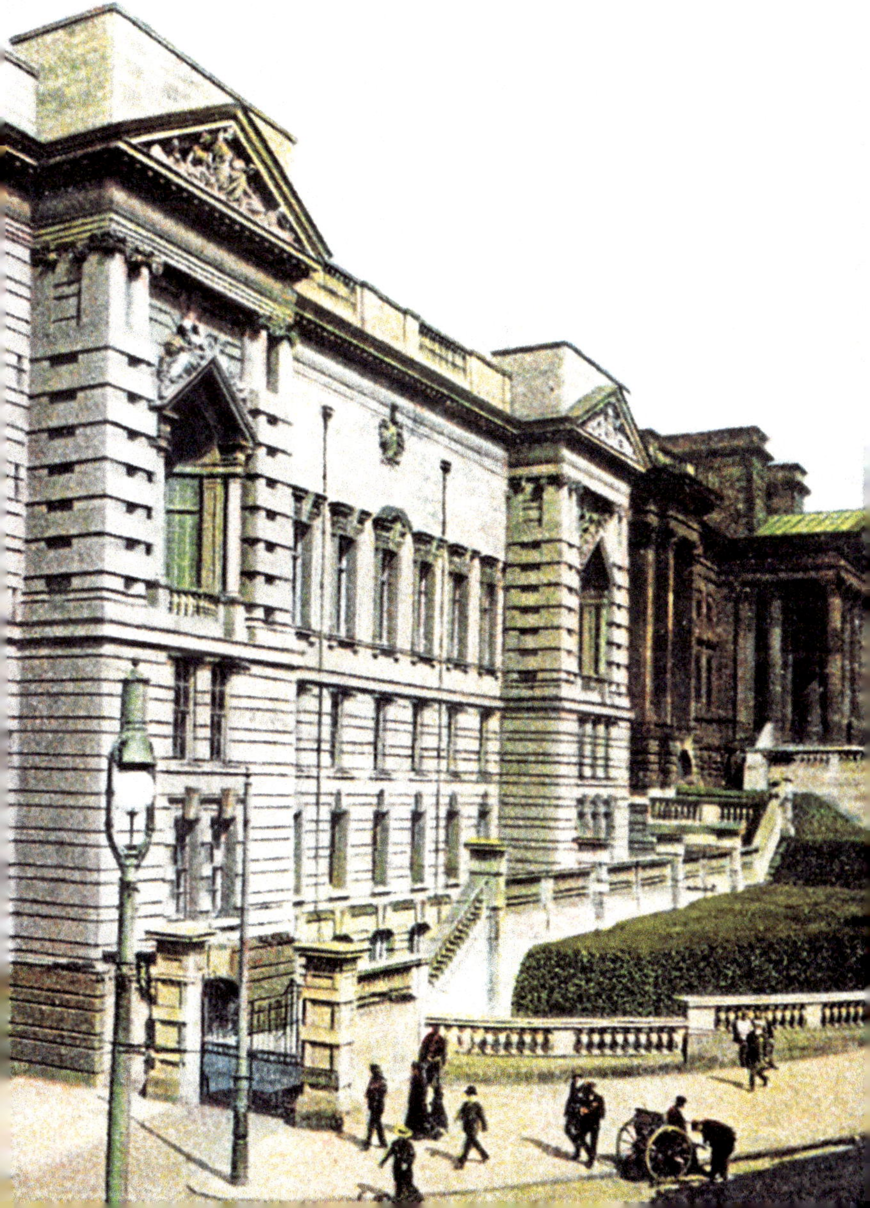

31. WALKER ART GALLERY

The Walker Art Gallery was designed by H. H. Vale and opened in 1877. It was a gift to the city by Sir A. B. Walker, a brewer during his mayoralty in 1873. Several attempts to organise public subscriptions to build an art gallery failed until Alderman Andrew Barclay Walker became mayor in 1873 and decided he would fund the building. The building was designed by Sherlock and Vale and was opened in 1877, enlarged by the addition of nine rooms in 1884; a further extension was later built in 1931–33.

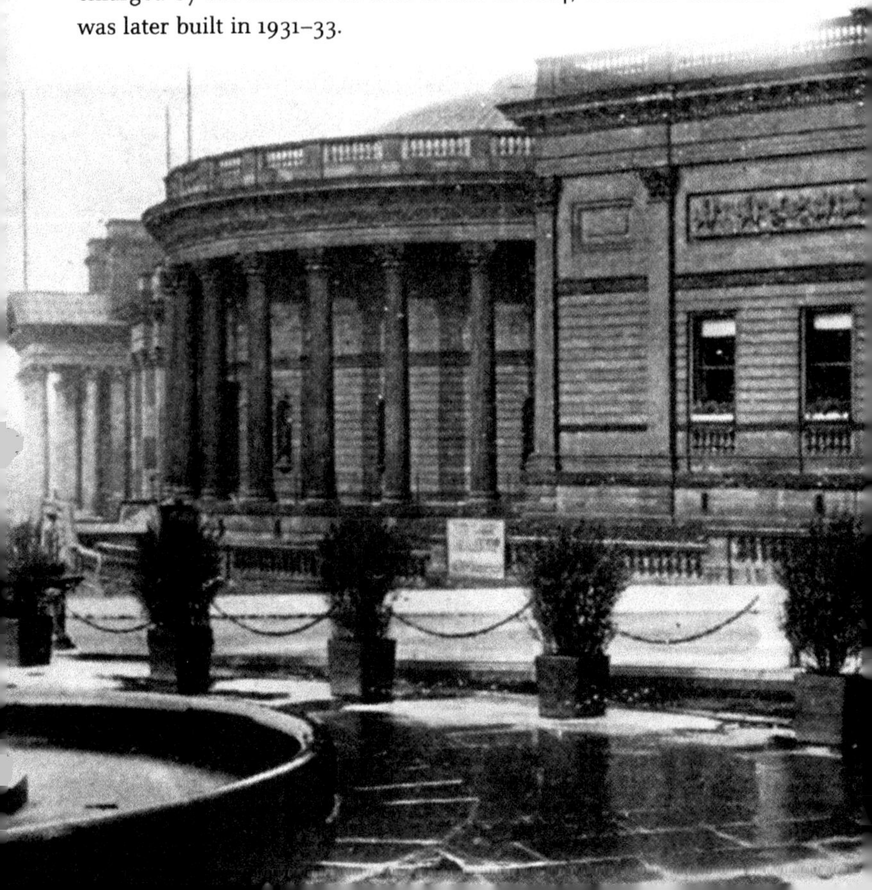

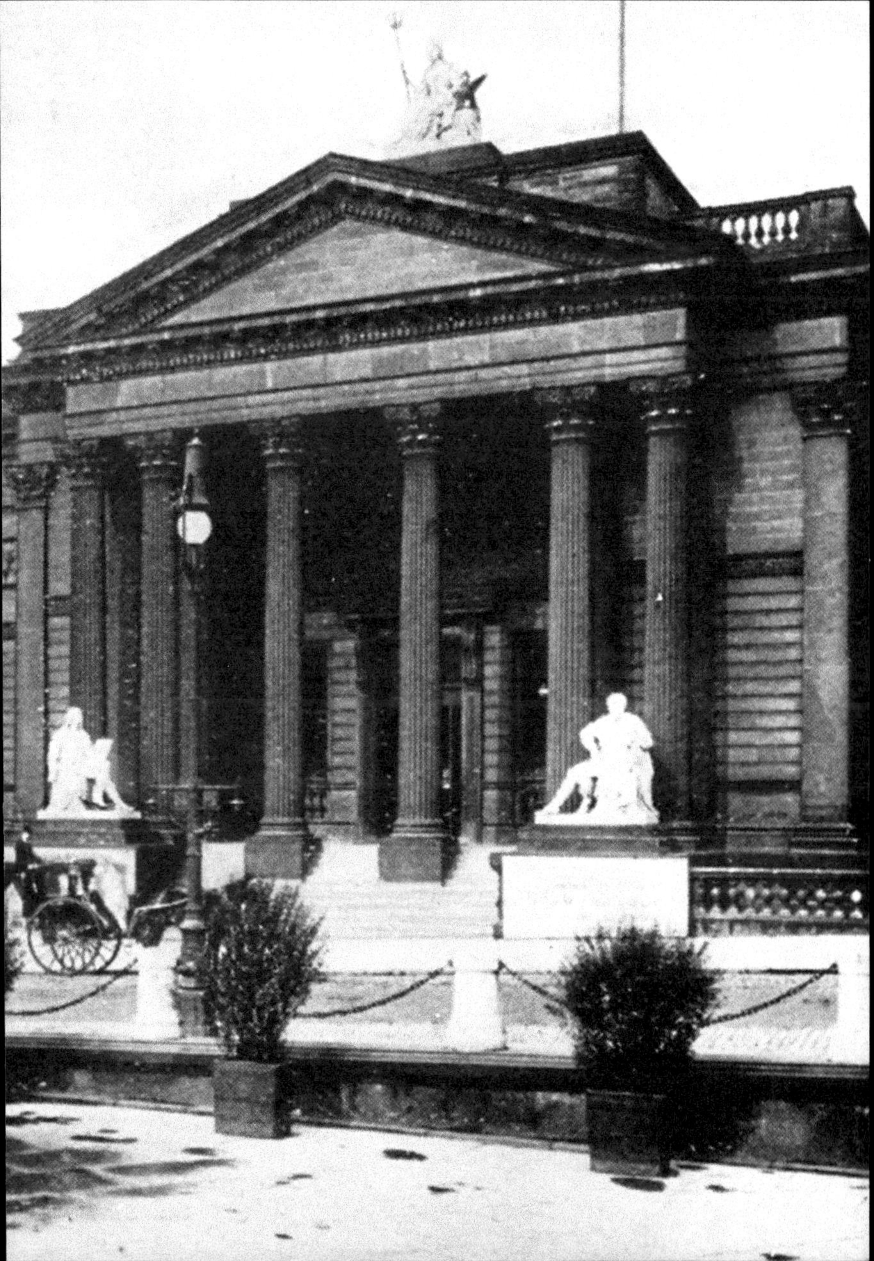

32. COUNTY SESSIONS HOUSE

The County Sessions House was built between 1882 and 1884 for the use of the magistrates of the Kirkdale division of South West Lancashire. The magistrates heard cases involving non-capital offences and the courts compliment the law courts in St Georges Hall. It is of Composite Classic architecture and the principal front has a portico of double columns. It was designed by F. & G. Holme, housing three courtrooms and attendant facilities, from a barrister library to cells. The Steble Fountain is in William Brown Street and was designed by W. Cunliffe. It was erected in 1879 and comprises of a circular stone basin with a bronze centrepiece of figures representing the four seasons. It was gifted to the city by Colonel R. F. Steble, who was mayor of Liverpool in 1874–75.

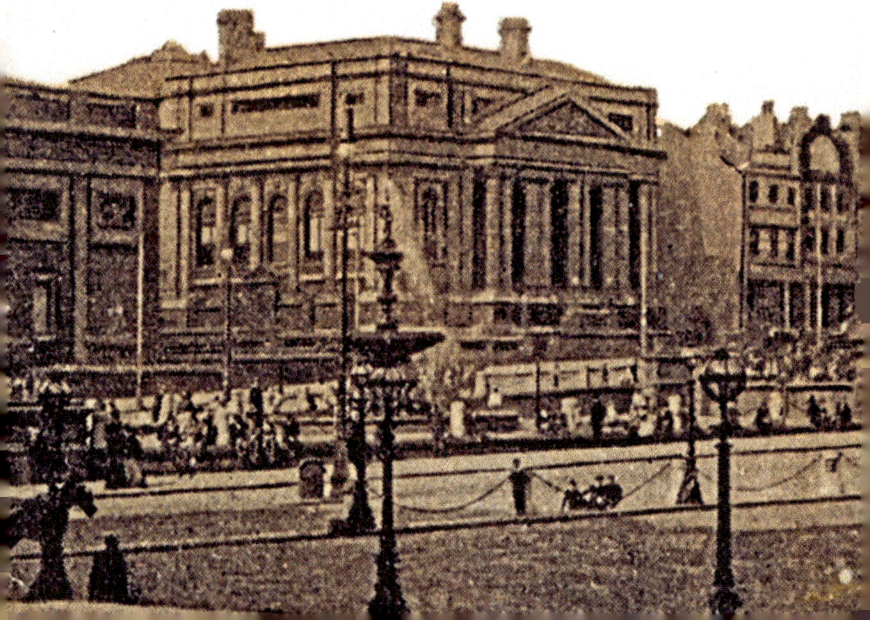

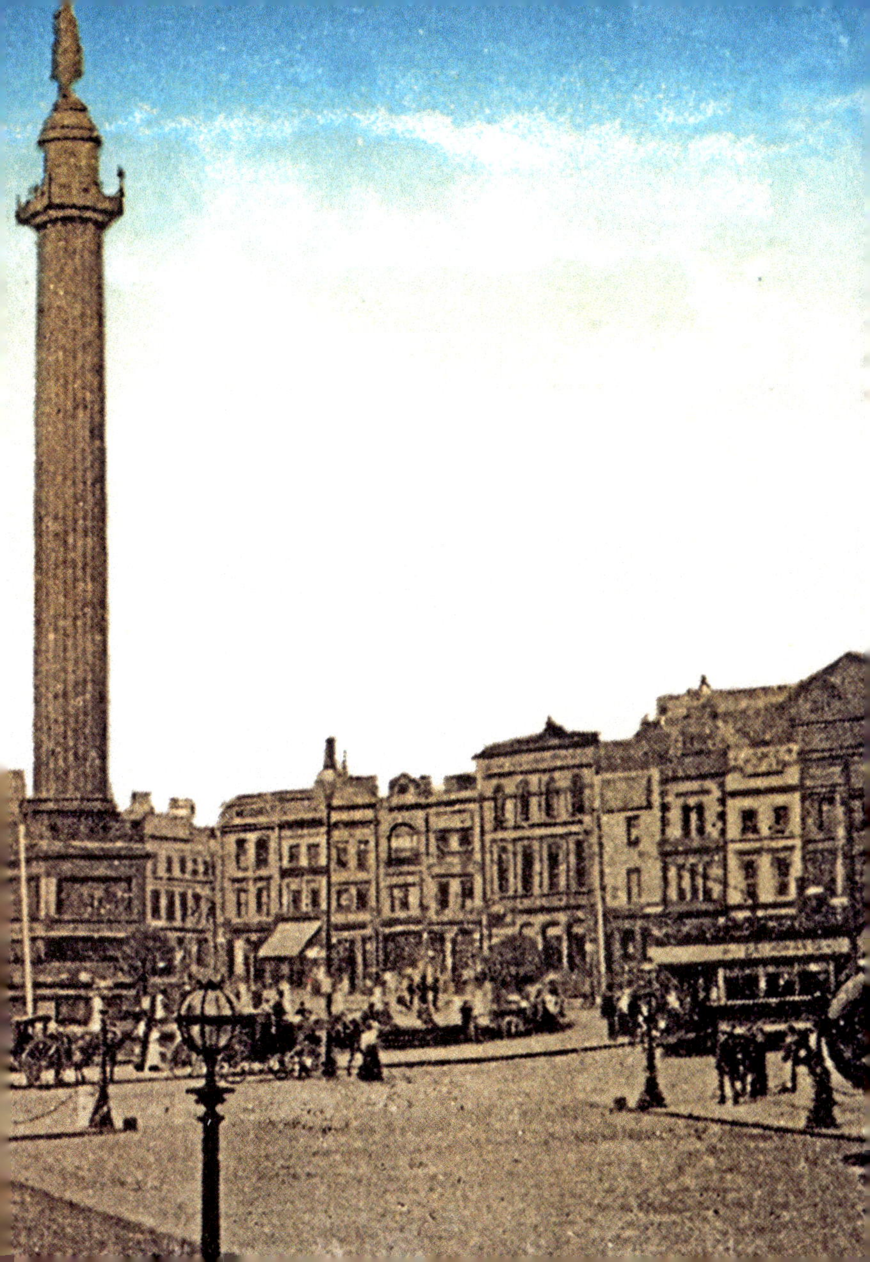

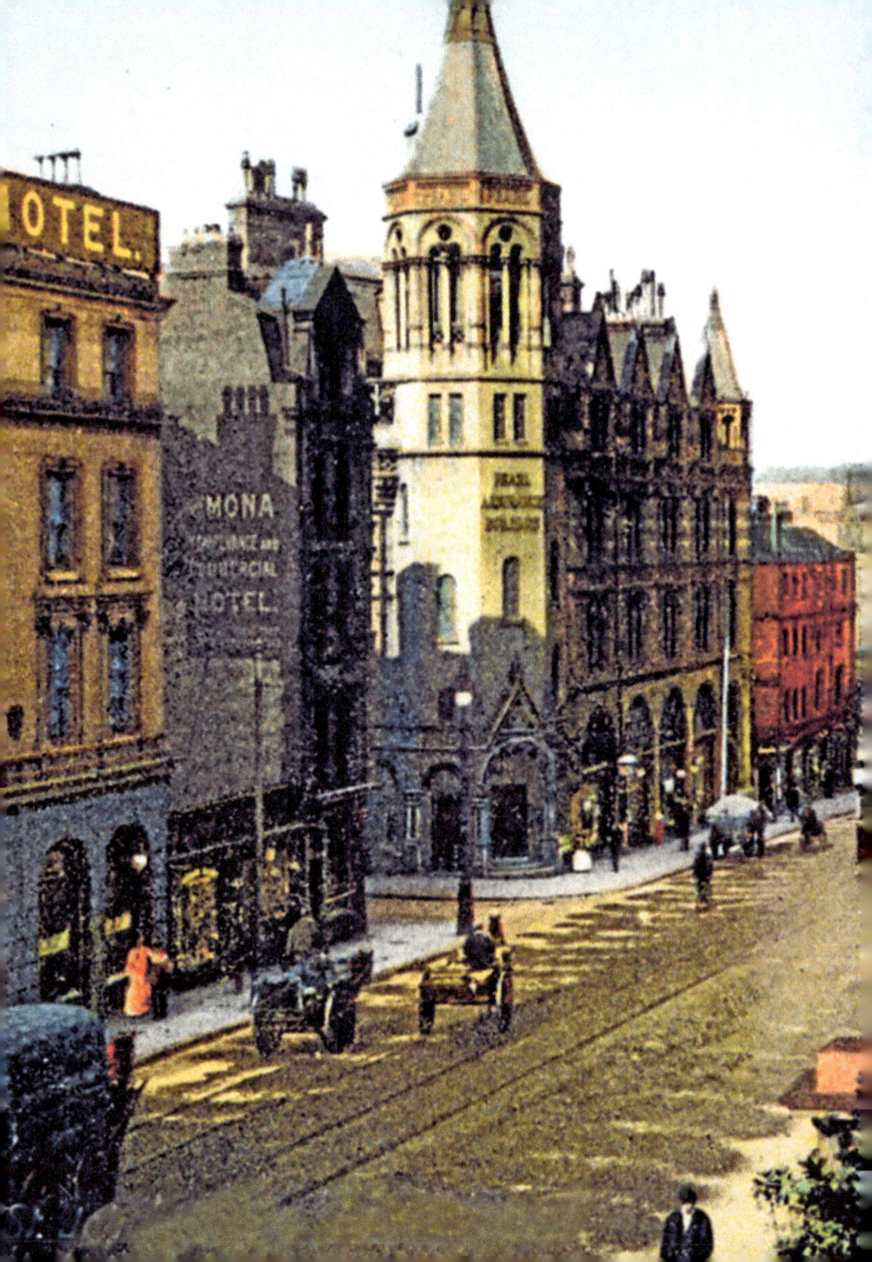
OTEL.
MONA
HOTEL.

33. ST JOHN'S GARDENS

St John's Garden was built on the site of St John's Church, which stood there from 1783 to 1887 and was demolished in 1888. The lane occupied part of what was the 'great heath' of Liverpool, which existed until the mid-eighteenth century, and the gardens are enclosed by a massive wall that runs around the 3.25 acres of lawns, trees, flowers and plants. The land sloped upwards and was exposed to the winds, making it ideal for windmills. Liverpool's first general infirmary was built on the site in 1749 and the Seaman's Hospital three years later, a dispensary was built in 1778 and an asylum in 1789. As well as windmills there were rope works, potteries, a marble yard and a row of lime kilns. The churchyard contained the graves of many French prisoners of the Napoleonic War who died in captivity in Liverpool. The gardens were laid out by Thomas Shelmerdine, the city surveyor, and were opened in 1904. The garden contains several monuments including the Gladstone Monument, which was erected in 1904.

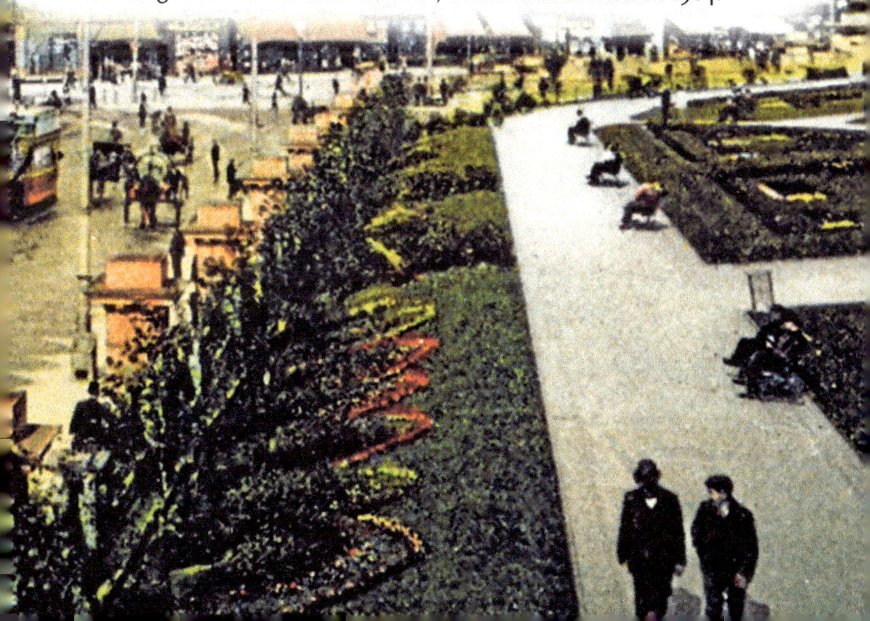

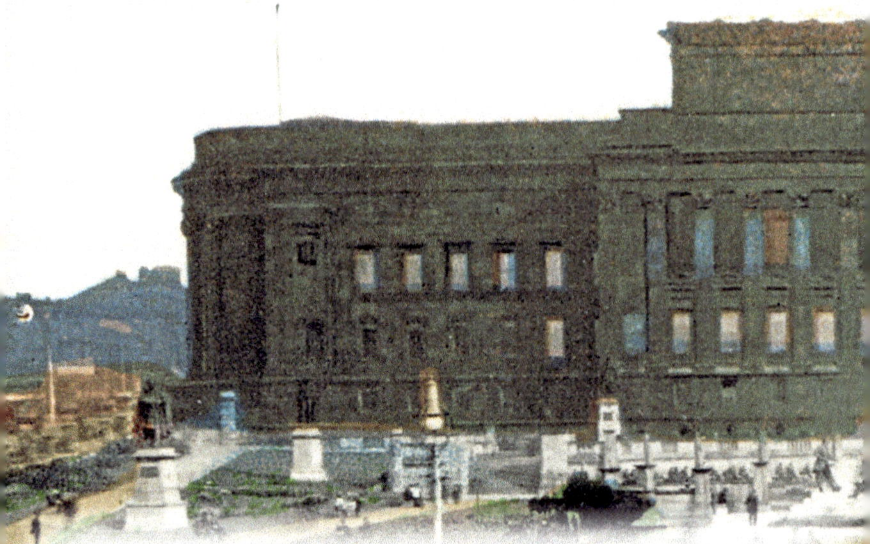

34. ST GEORGE'S HALL

St Georges Hall was opened on 18 September 1854 at a cost of £380,000. It was designed by Harvey Lonsdale Elmes and built on the site of the Liverpool Infirmary. A company was formed in 1836 to raise subscriptions for a hall that would be used for festivals, concerts, dinners and meetings. Shares were offered at £25 each and in 1838 the foundation stone was laid to commemorate the coronation of Queen Victoria. Elmes included provision for an assize court in the plans for the building and work began in 1841. Elmes was only twenty-four years of age when his design was adopted; he died in 1847 at the age of thirty-three. The work was continued with John Weightman and Robert Rawlinson as the structural engineers and Sir Charles Cockerell was appointed as architect in 1851.

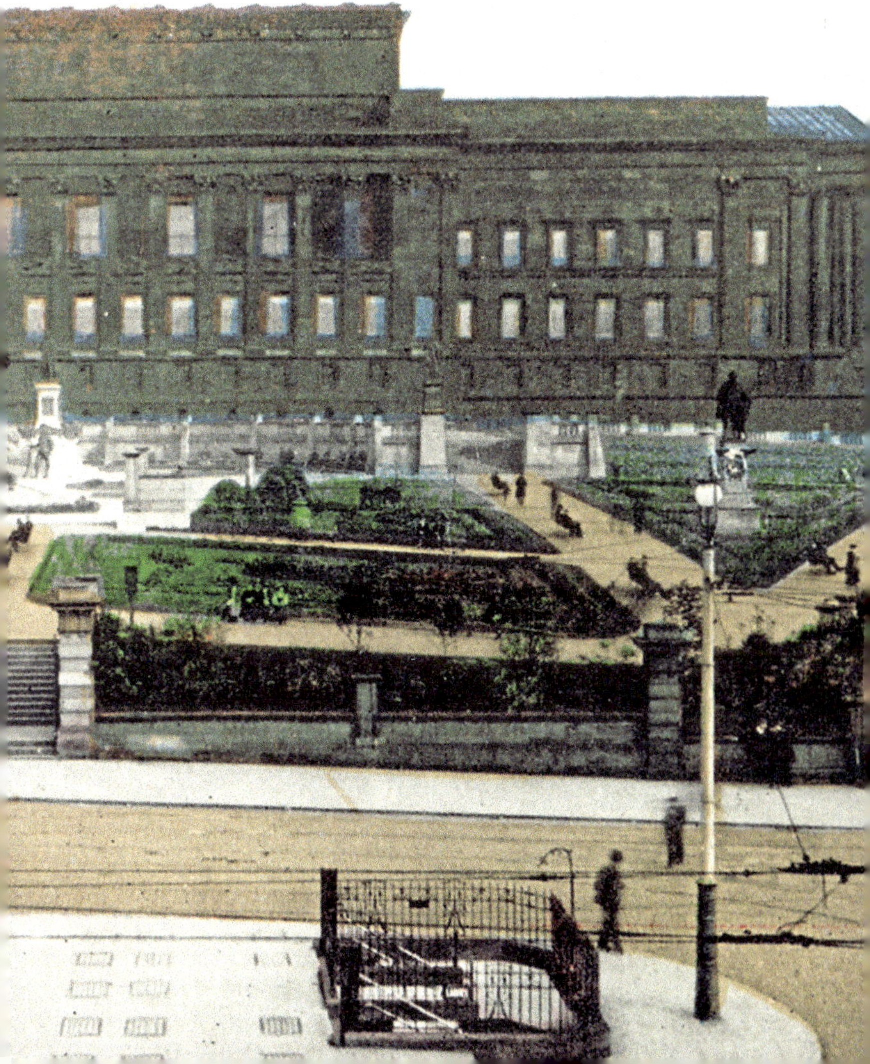

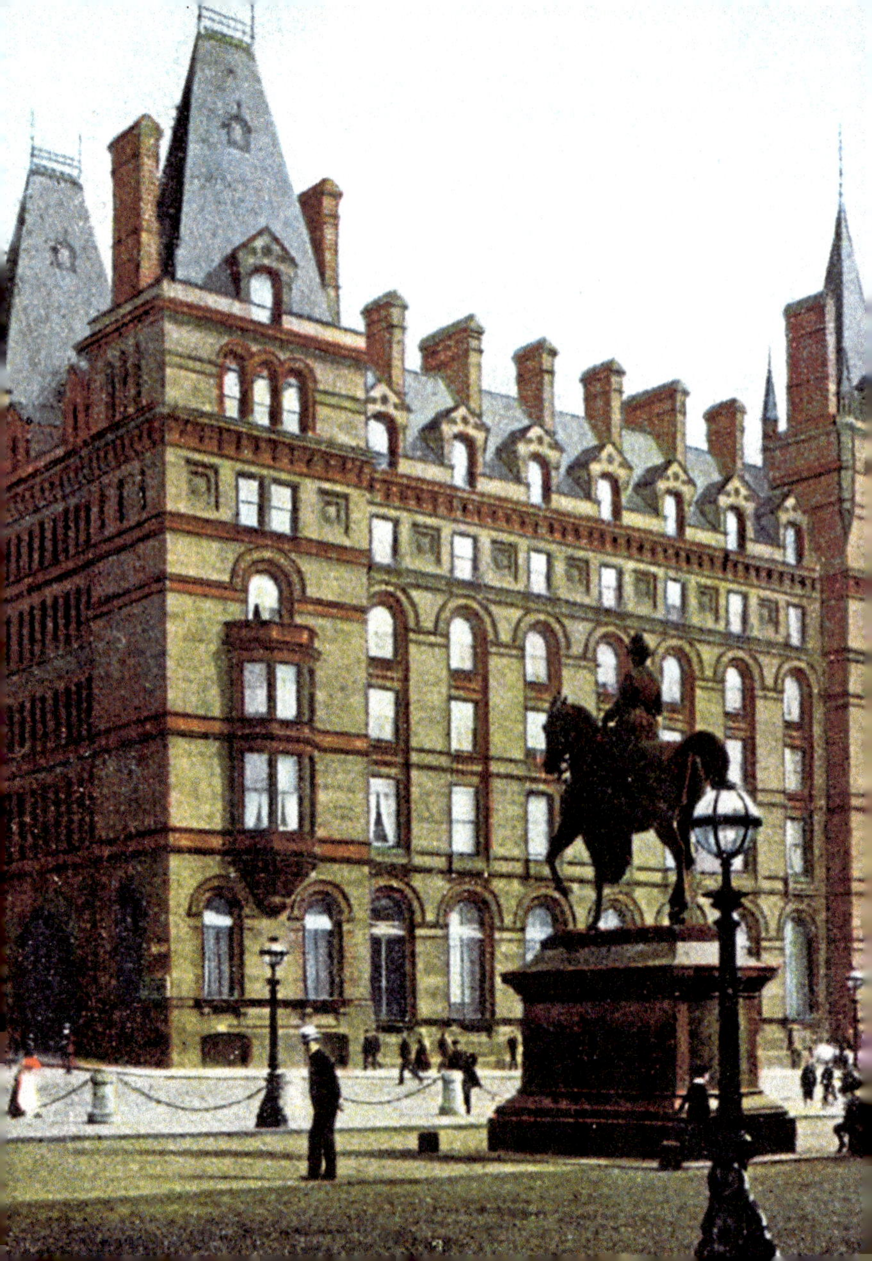

35. NORTH WESTERN HOTEL

The former North Western Hotel in Lime Street was opened as a 330-room hotel in 1871. It was designed by Alfred Waterhouse, who was also responsible for the Prudential Building in Dale Street and the Natural History Museum in London. The building is built in the French Renaissance style and is faced with Caen and Storton stone. It has five storeys plus dormers, with pavilion-roofed corner towers and two further towers with short spires flanking the central entrance. It was purchased by the John Moores University in 1994 for £6 million and now provides accommodation for students in 246 apartments.

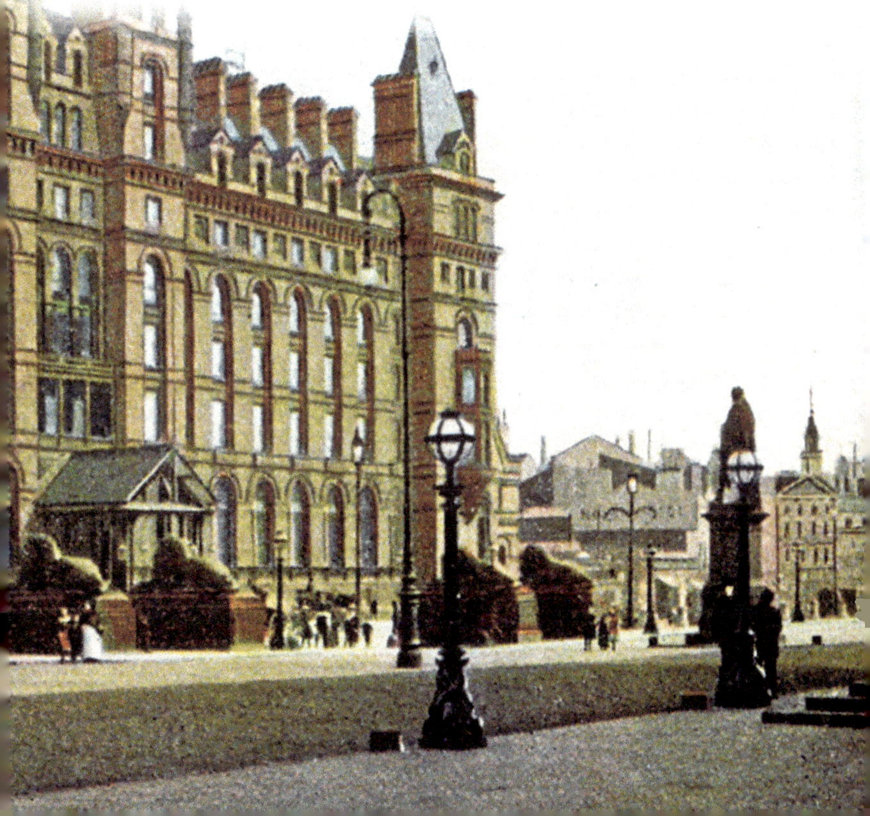

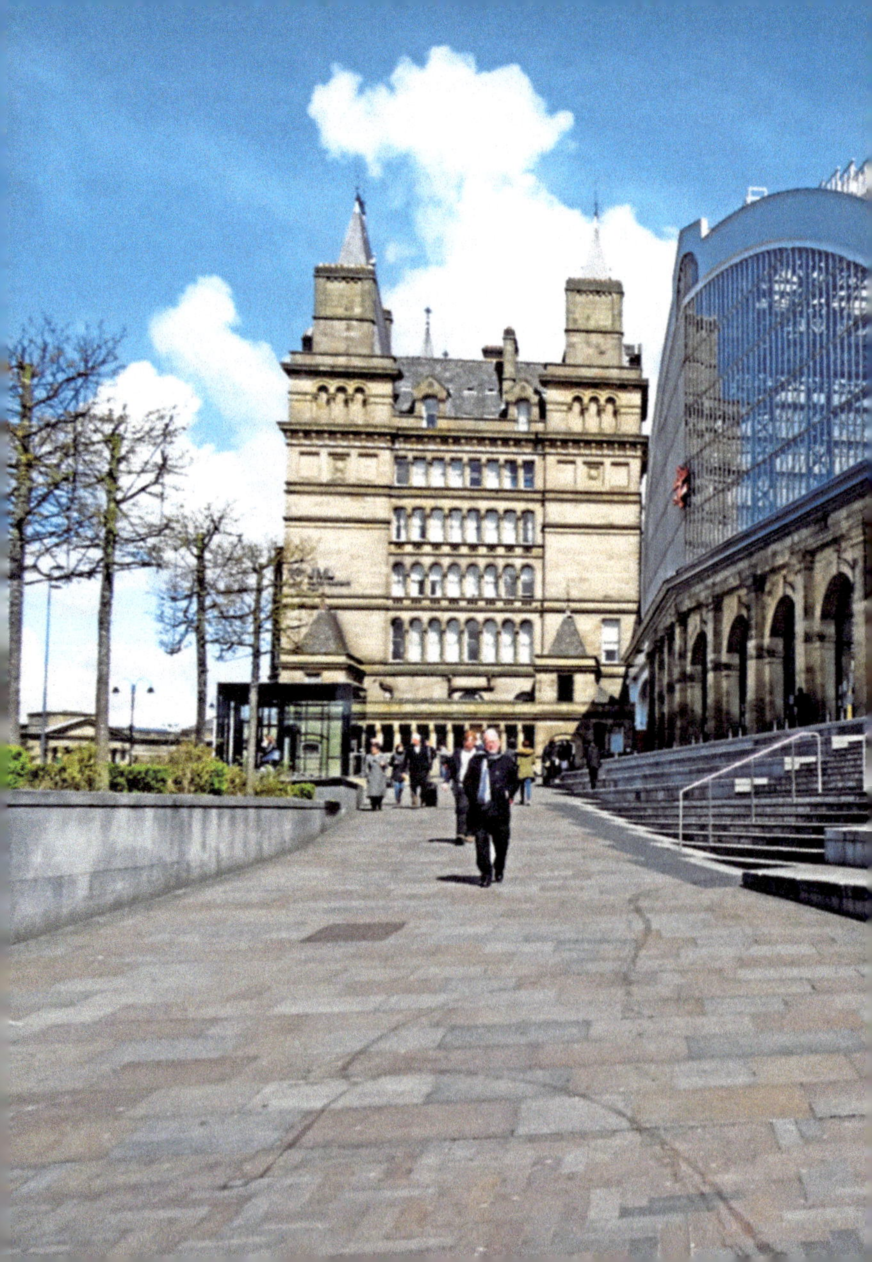

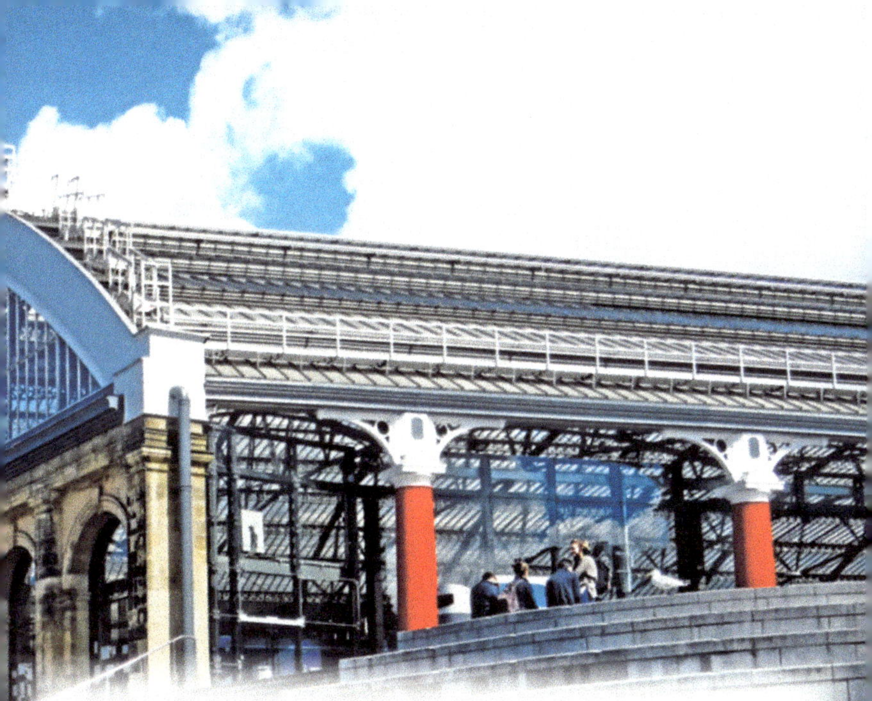

36. LIME STREET STATION

The opening of the line from Liverpool to Manchester in 1830 formed the beginning of the local railway system. The original terminus of the Liverpool & Manchester Railway was at Crown Street, Edge Hill, just outside the city centre. Lime Street Station was adequate for its purpose when it was built but was soon enlarged, with the work necessitating the destruction of whole streets and the removal and rebuilding of St Simon's Church. Construction of the new station began in October 1833 when the land was purchased from Liverpool Corporation for £9,000. Prior to the opening of the station a tunnel was constructed between Edge Hill and Lime Street. Cunningham and Holme were the architects for the project and the station was opened in August 1836, with the work being completed the following year.

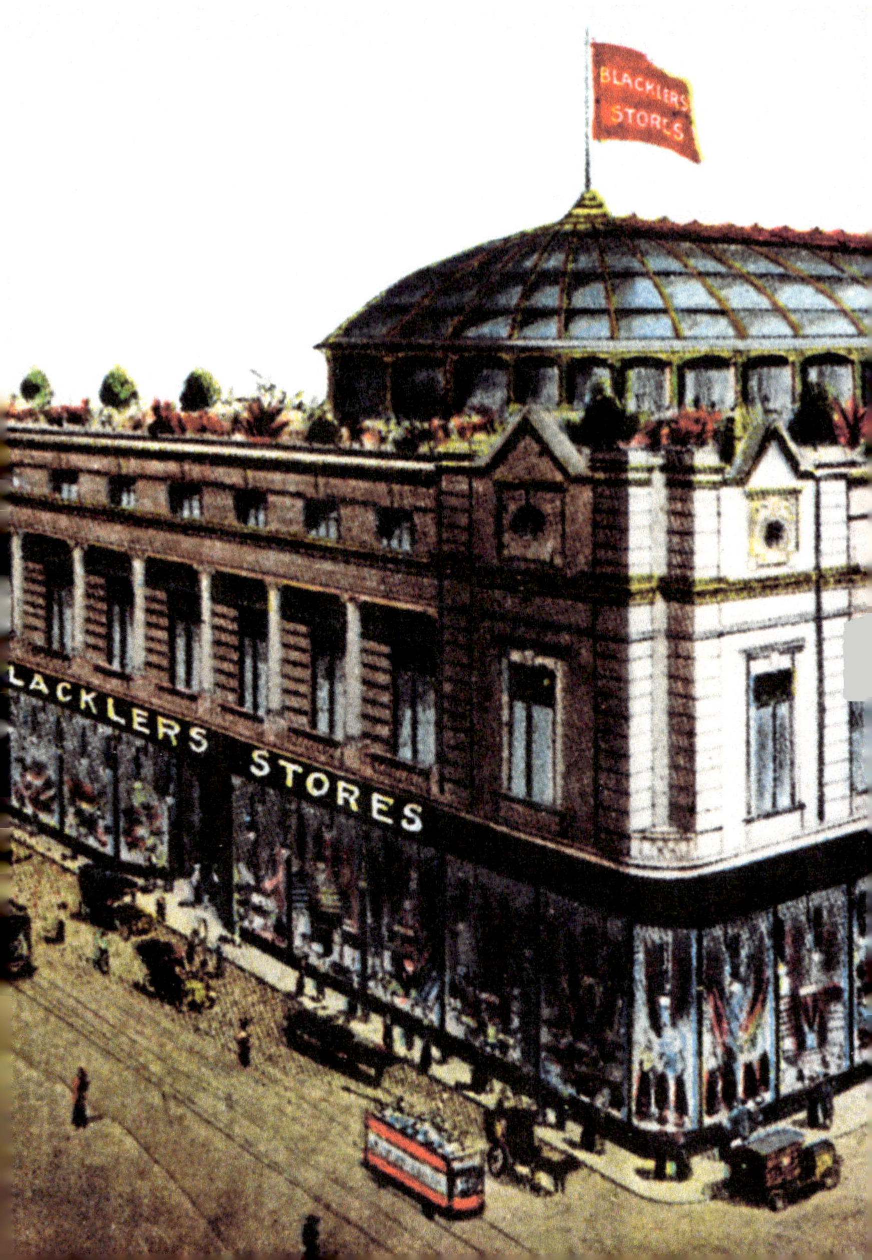
BLACKLERS
STORES
LACKLERS STORES

37. BLACKLERS

Blacklers department store was situated on the corner of Elliot Street and Great Charlotte Street. It was founded by Richard Blackler and A. B. Wallis in the early twentieth century. When Richard died in 1919, his wife Margaret became managing partner and the store became so successful that it employed over 1,000 people at its peak. The building was damaged in May 1941 and the company operated from premises in Church Street and Bold Street. The store reopened in 1953 and operated until its closure in 1988

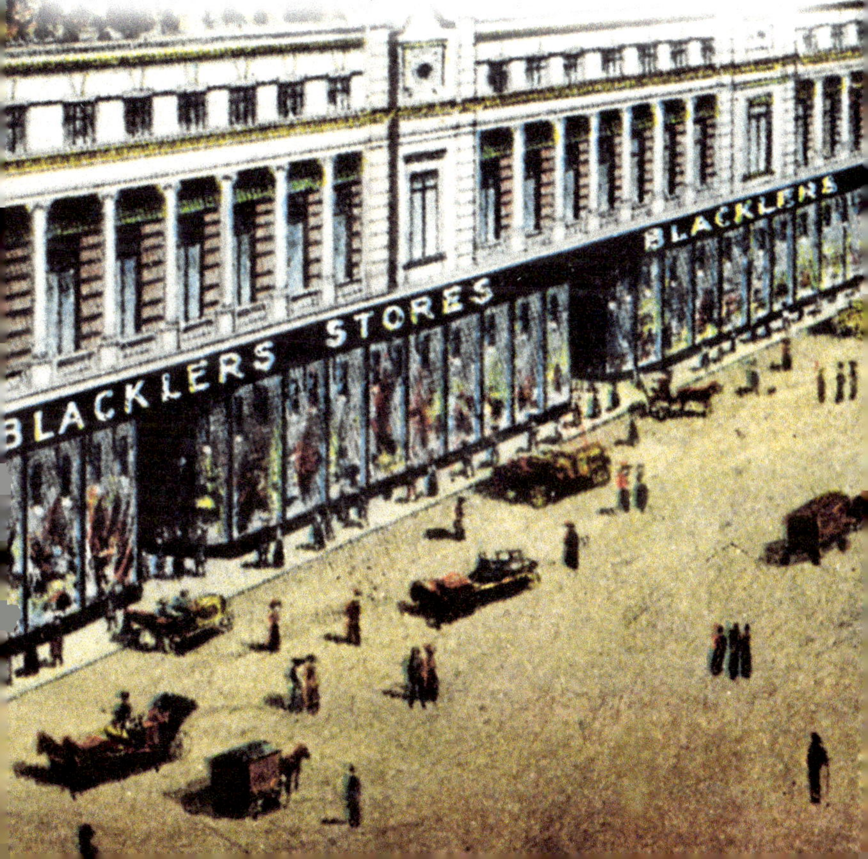

38. ST PETER'S CHURCH, CHURCH STREET

Liverpool became a separate parish from Walton in 1699 and £400 was raised to build a new church, which was to be dedicated to St Peter. The church was designed by John Moffat and it was built at a cost of £4000, then consecrated on 29 June 1704. The last service took place in the church in September 1919 and the building was demolished in 1922.

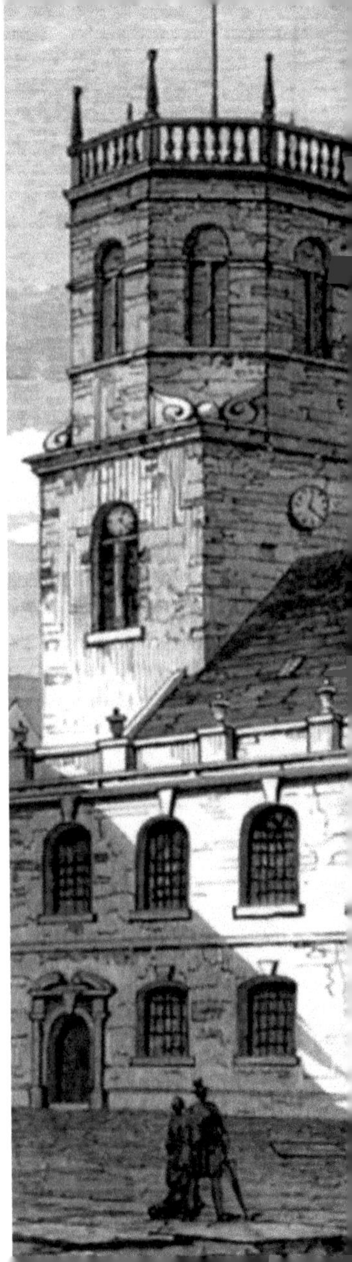

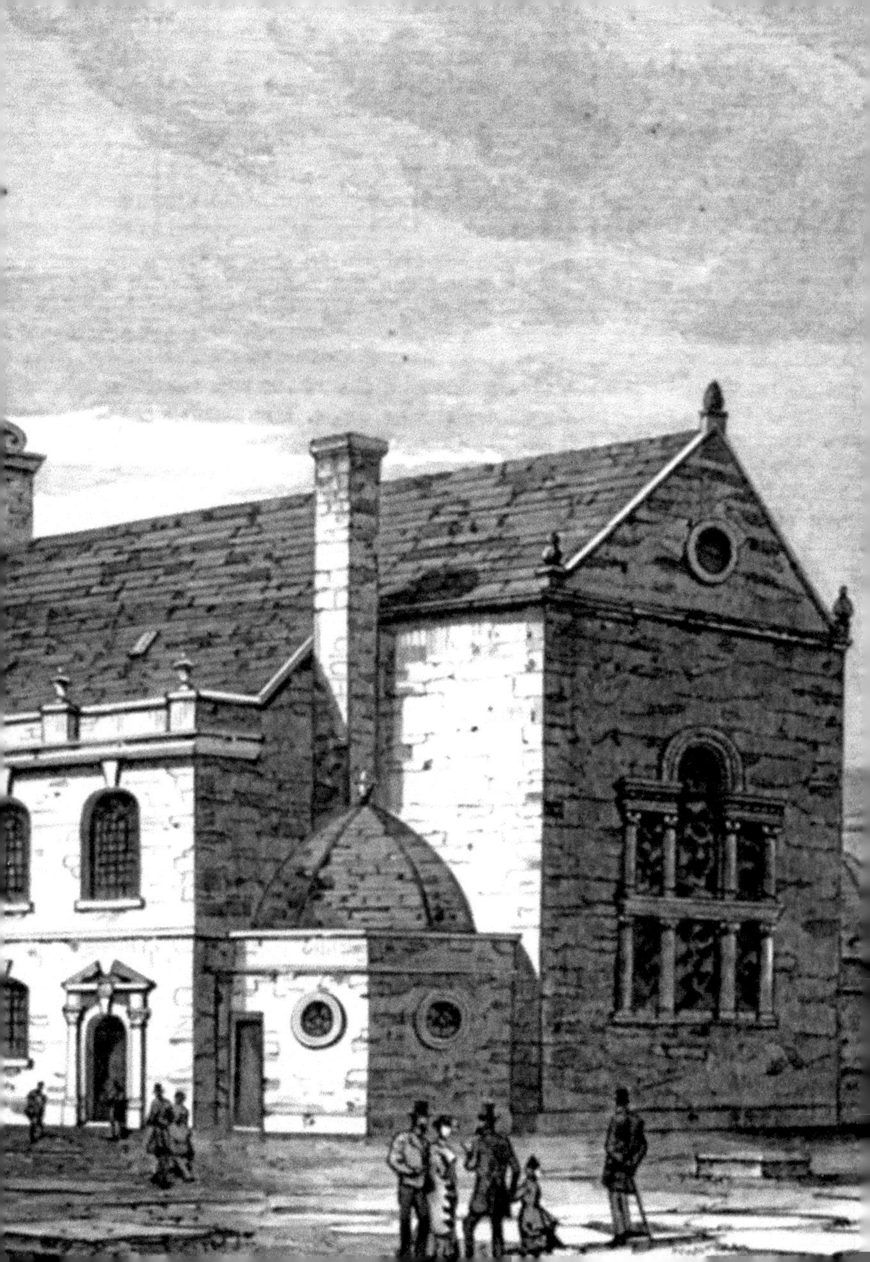

39. LIVERPOOL BLUE COAT SCHOOL

The Liverpool Blue Coat School was founded in 1708 by master mariner Bryan Blundell and Revd Robert Styth, the then rector of Liverpool. The Revd Styth organised 'a place where poor children could be accommodated, cared and learn to read, write and cast accounts'. The financial backing was provided by Blundell. The original building was in School Lane and in 1719 a new building was erected in the style of Queen Anne. When Revd Styth died in 1713, Blundell noticed that the poverty of the time was causing the children to neglect their school work and he changed the school into a boarding school, providing food, drink and lodging to the pupils. The school was extended in 1718 and the finance was again provided by Blundell. By the end of the nineteenth century it was clear that a new school building was required and this was completed at Wavertree in 1906. It was then used by the Sandon Studios Society of Arts and it was acquired by the Bluecoat Society for the Arts in 1927. The Bluecoat Gallery was formed in 1968 and the building in School Lane is now the centre of Liverpool's artistic life.

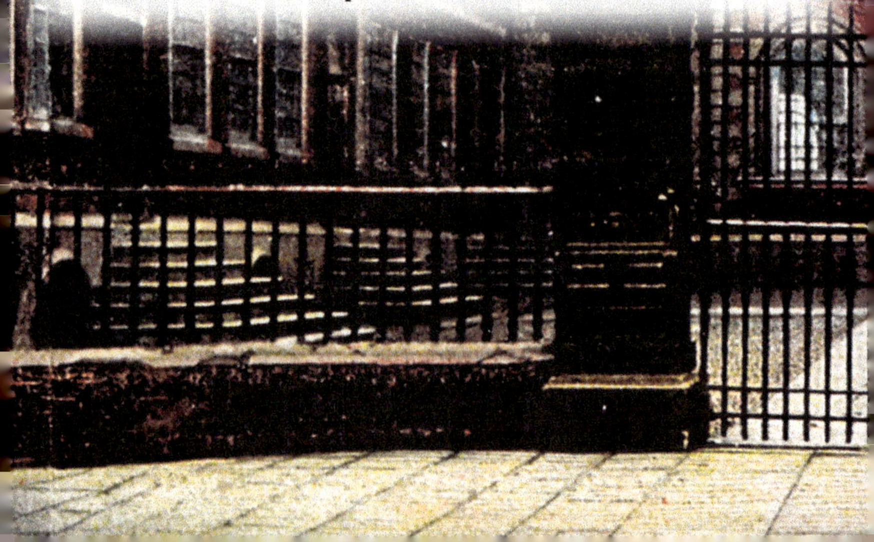

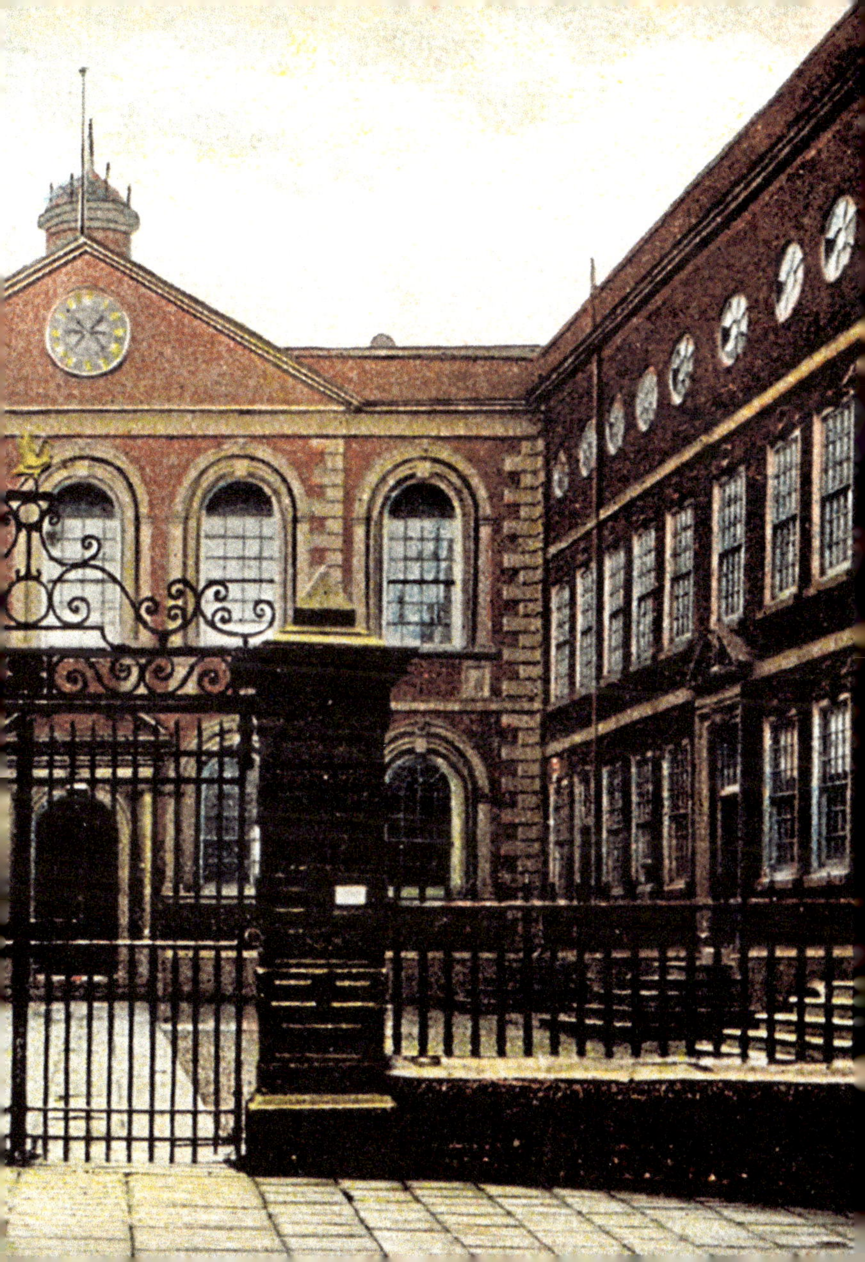

40. LEWIS'S

David Lewis opened his first store in 1856, selling men's and boy's clothing, adding women's clothing from 1864. He added shoes in 1874, tobacco in 1879, and a Christmas grotto in 1879. A store was opened in Manchester in 1877 and another in Birmingham in 1885. The store in Manchester included a full-scale ballroom on the fifth floor, which was also used for exhibitions. In 1879, Lewis's opened one of the world's first Christmas grottoes in Lewis's Bon Marche, Church Street, Liverpool and it was named Christmas Fairyland. The Manchester branch ceased trading in 2002 and last store to operate was at Liverpool. However, the company went into administration on 28 February 2007, and the store was sold to Vergo Retail Limited. This store continued to trade but it was announced that it would finally close on 29 May 2010.

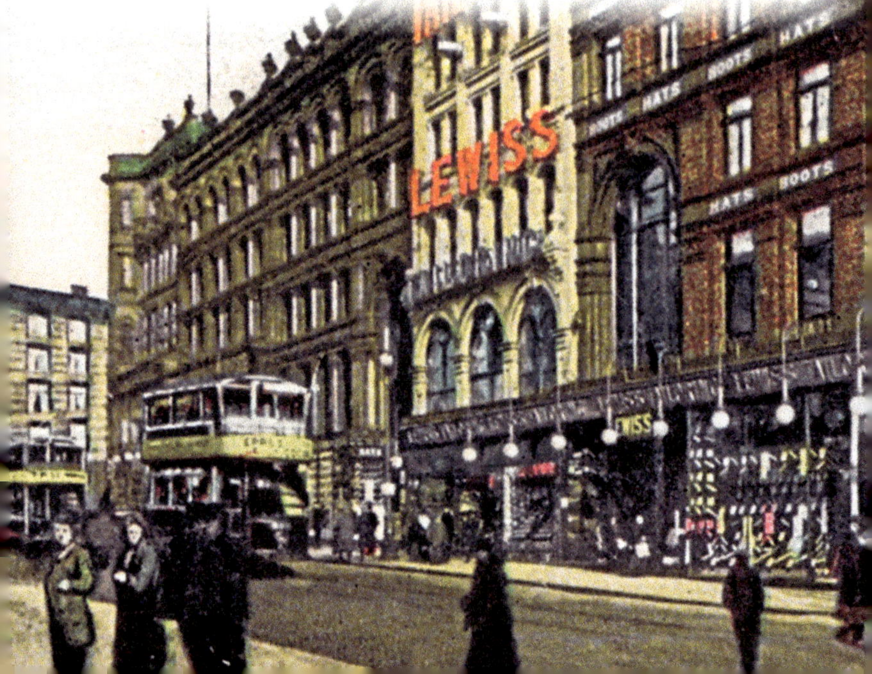

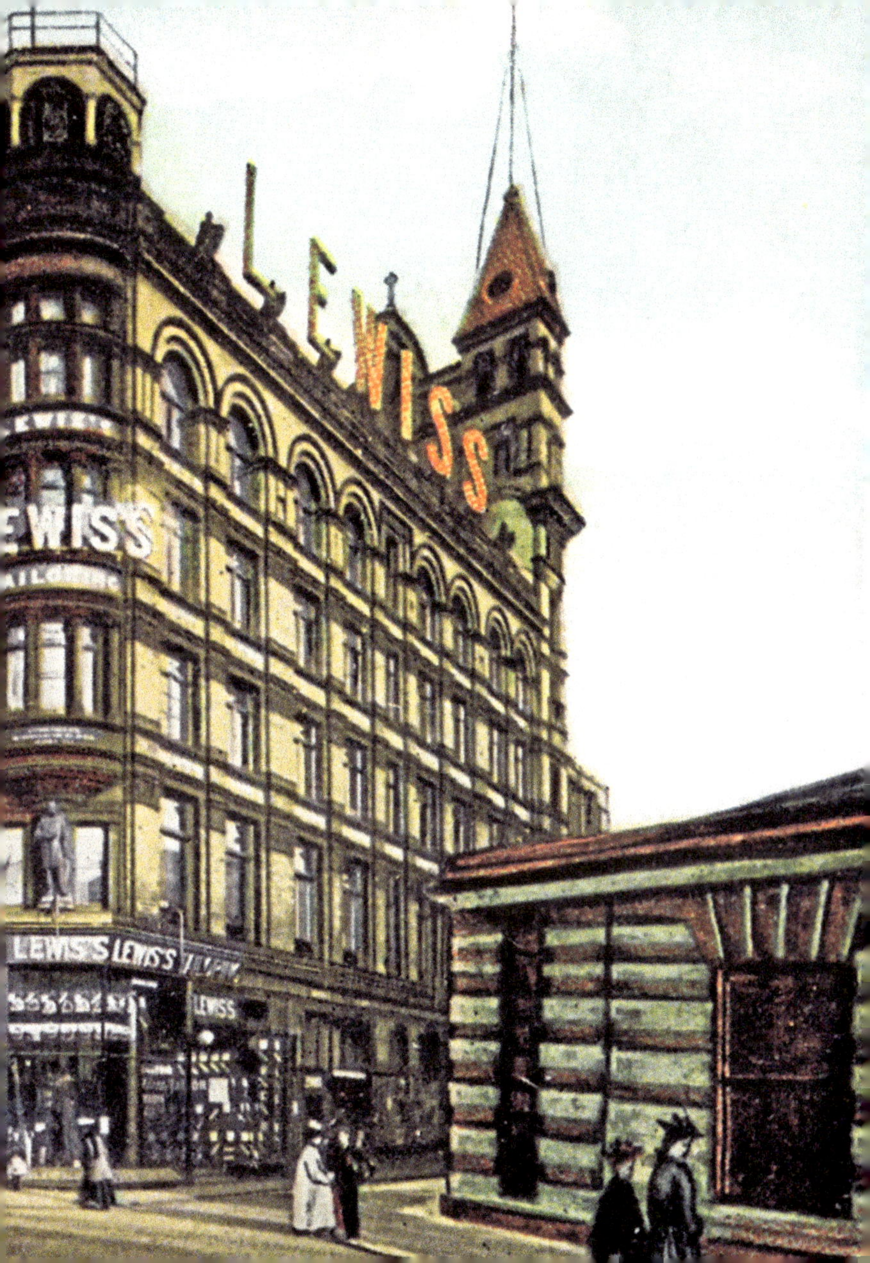
LEWISS
LEWIS'S LEWIS'S
LEWIS'S

41. ST PETER'S CHURCH, SEEL STREET

St Peter's Church was opened on 7 September 1788 by Revd A. B. MacDonald of the Order of St Benedict. The *Liverpool Advertiser* reported that, 'On Sunday last, a new Roman Catholic Chapel in Seel Street, was opened with High Mass, and a sermon by the Reverend Mr McDonald.' The first baptisms were performed on 28 September and the first entry in the baptism book was for Mary, daughter of John and Mary Goosse. On 1 April 1789, a perpetual lease was granted by the Corporation, 'to Father McDonald and successors of the site of St Peter's Chapel, so long as a place of worship'. In 1976 the church was transferred to the Polish community, and for a short time was known as Our Lady of Czestochowa. The church was deconsecrated in 1993. A bar and restaurant called Alma de Cuba was opened in the building of St Peter's Church in 2005.

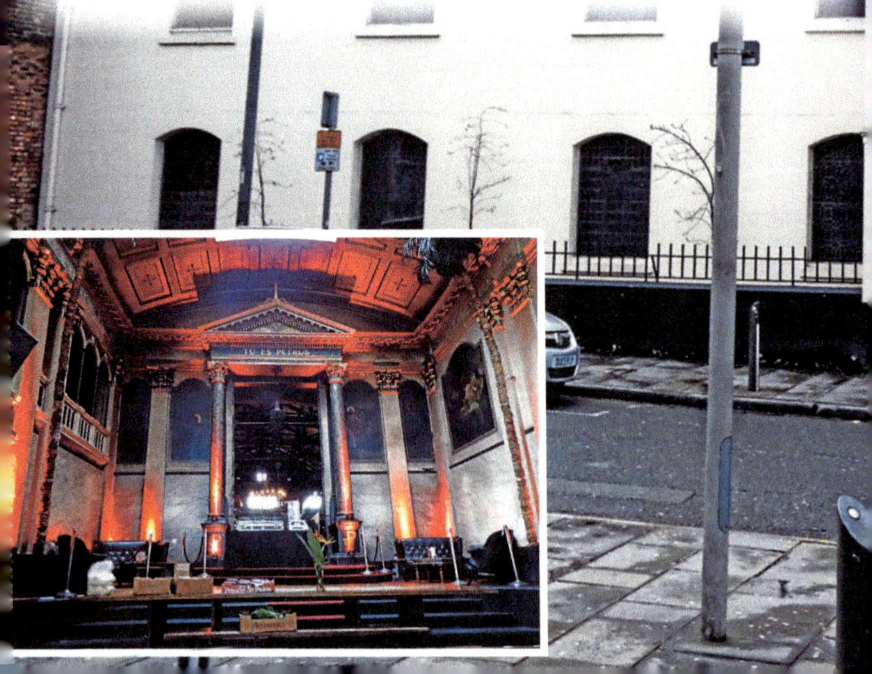

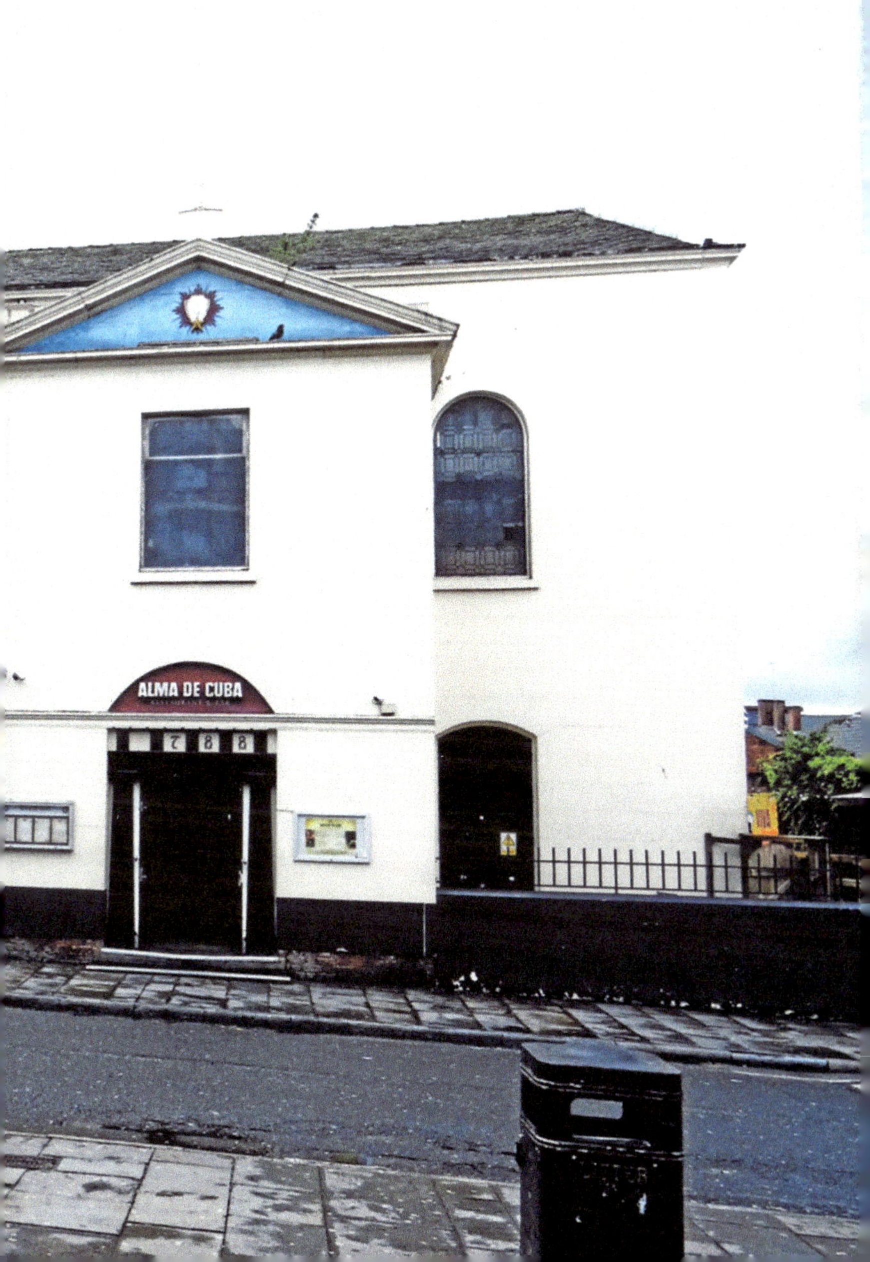
ALMA DE CUBA
7 8 8

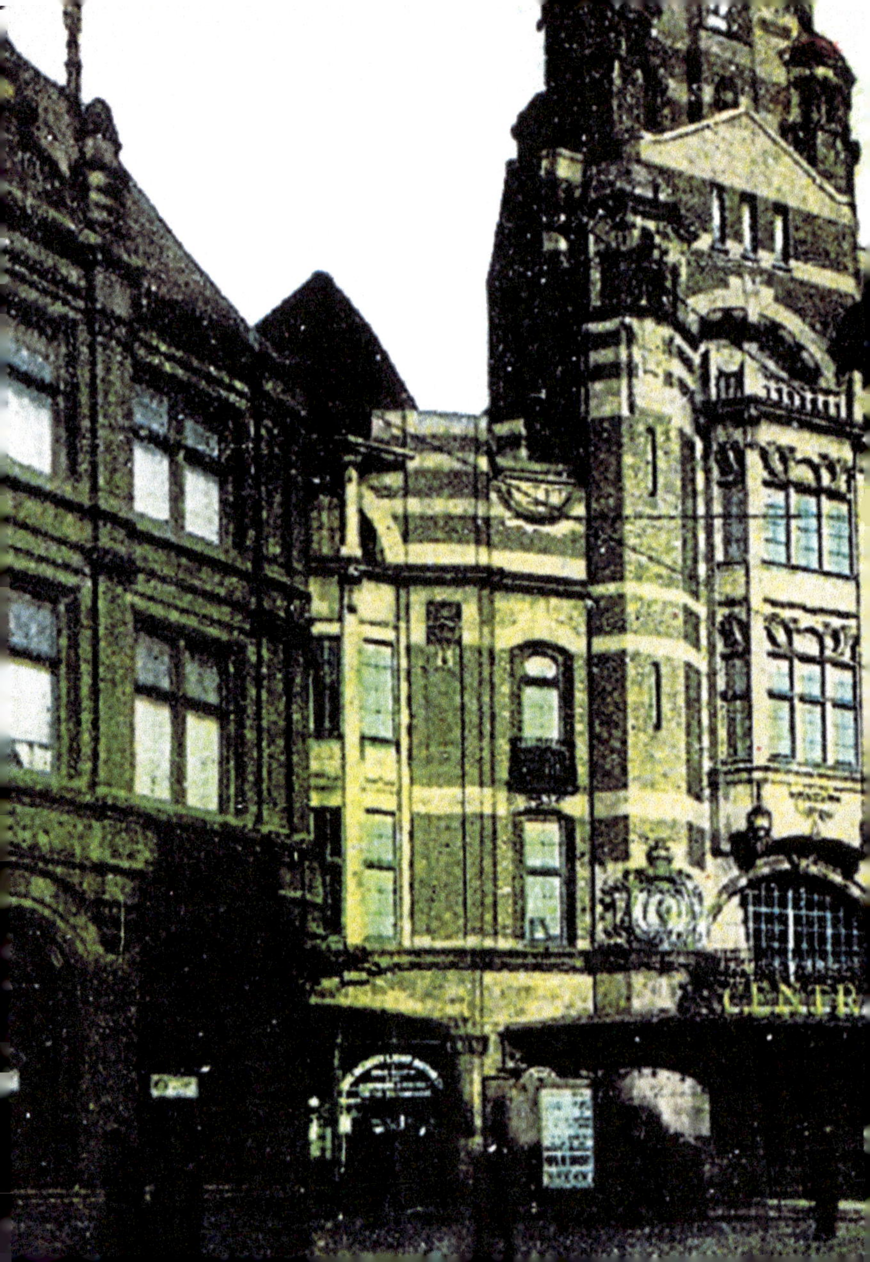

42. CENTRAL HALL

The Central Hall was a Wesleyan Methodist church, which was opened on the 5 December 1905 and is now a Grade II-listed building. It was designed by Bradshaw & Glass of Bolton. It was built on the site a Unitarian chapel that dated from 1790 as a memorial to Charles Garrett, who had died in 1900. The graveyard of the chapel contained the grave of the historian and philanthropist Roscoe. Central Hall provided seats for 3,576 people: 1,788 in the large hall, 102 in the orchestra, 858 in the stalls and 828 in the balcony. The building was sold in 1990 and in 1997–98 it underwent major restoration work and opened as a nightclub and bar, and has also been used by traders from Quiggin's.

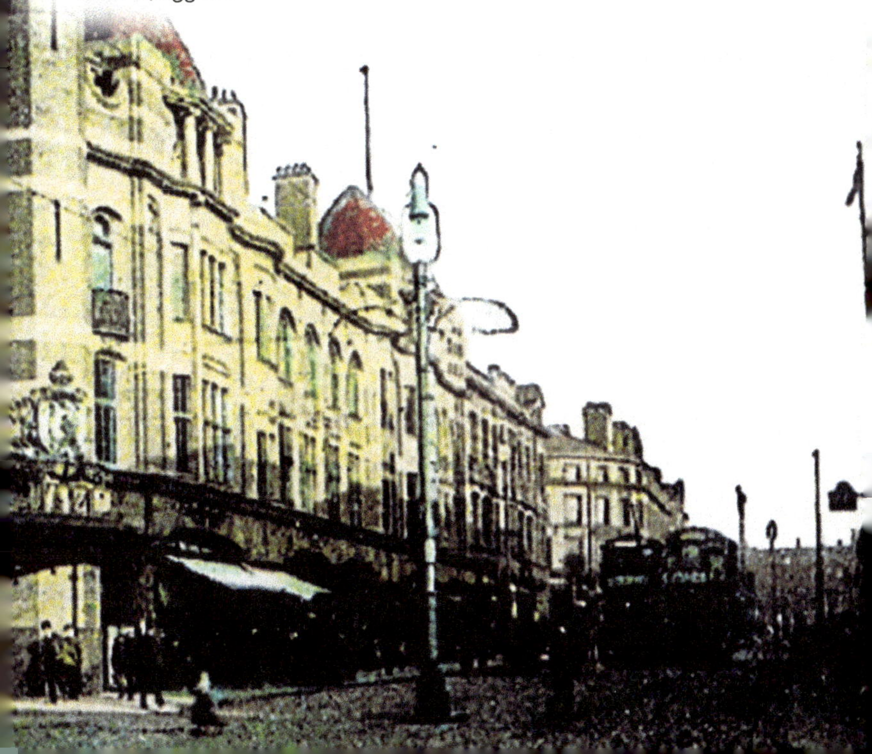

43. NO. 62 RODNEY STREET

No. 62 Rodney Street was built in 1796; it is the birthplace of William Ewart Gladstone, who was born there on 29 December 1809 and was the son of a prosperous merchant. The house originally stood detached, with a wing on either side, but one wing was later altered and converted to a separate dwelling. It is a large five-bay house, with the centre three bays projecting slightly and crowned by a pediment. Gladstone was educated at Eaton and the University of Oxford; he was elected to Parliament in 1832 as a Tory.

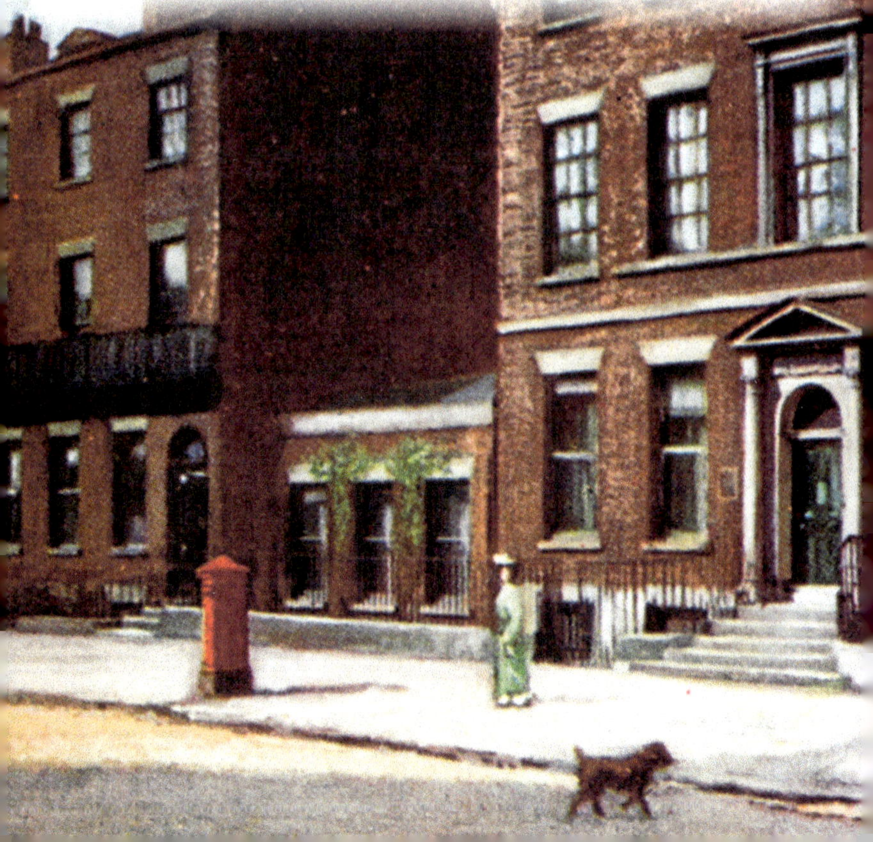

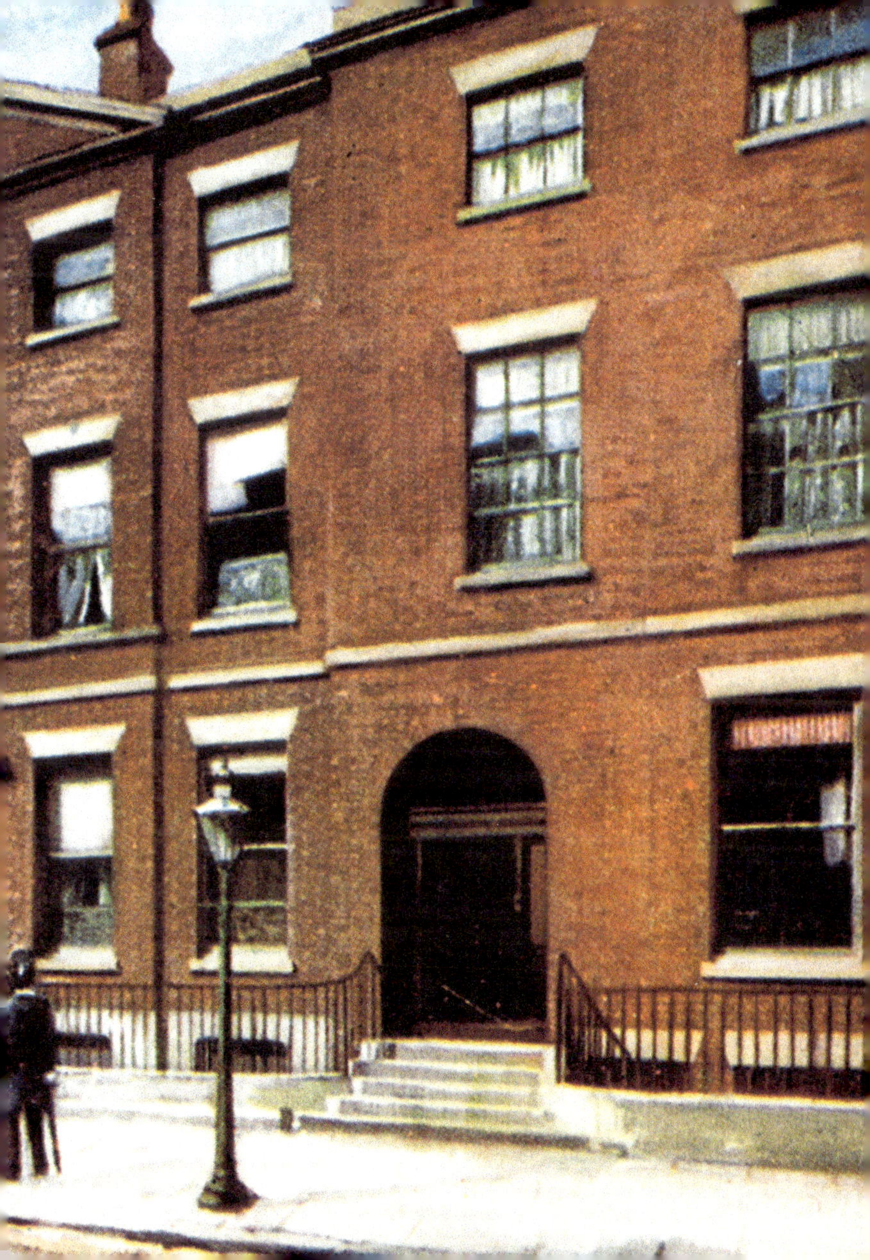

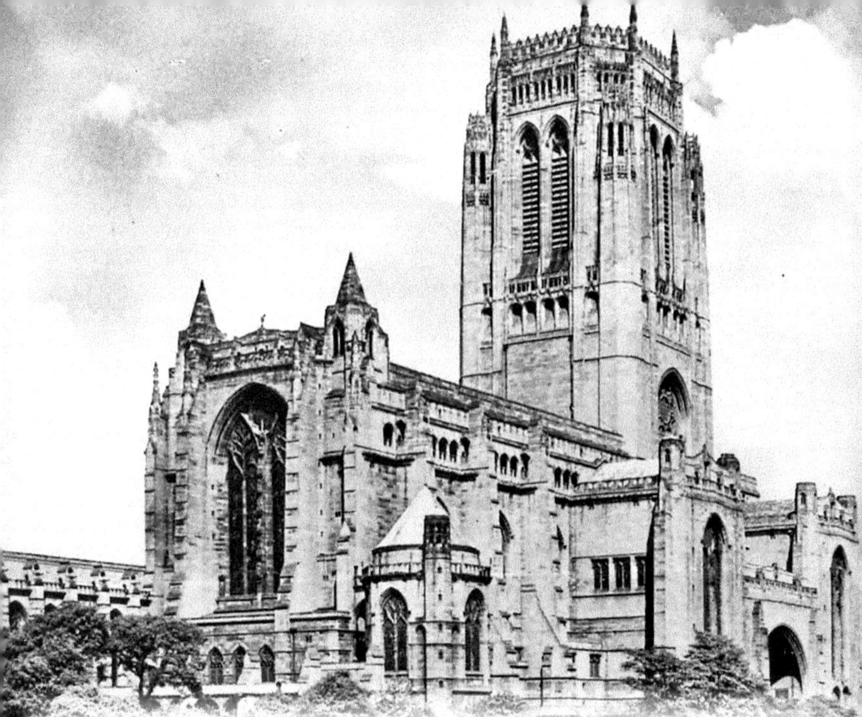

44. LIVERPOOL ANGLICAN CATHEDRAL

The Anglican Cathedral, built on St James' Mount, is the largest in the United Kingdom and the fifth largest in the world. The official name is the Cathedral Church of Christ in Liverpool and it is dedicated to Christ and the Blessed Virgin. The first bishop of Liverpool was the Rt Revd John Charles Ryle, who was installed in 1880 when the city did not have a cathedral, only the parish church of St Peter's. A competition to design a new cathedral attracted over 100 entries and Giles Gilbert Scott's design was chosen, with George F. Bodley to oversee the detailed architectural design and building work. The foundation stone was laid by Edward VII in 1904 and the Lady chapel was opened in 1910. The building was opened by Elizabeth II in October 1978, followed by a service of thanksgiving and dedication.

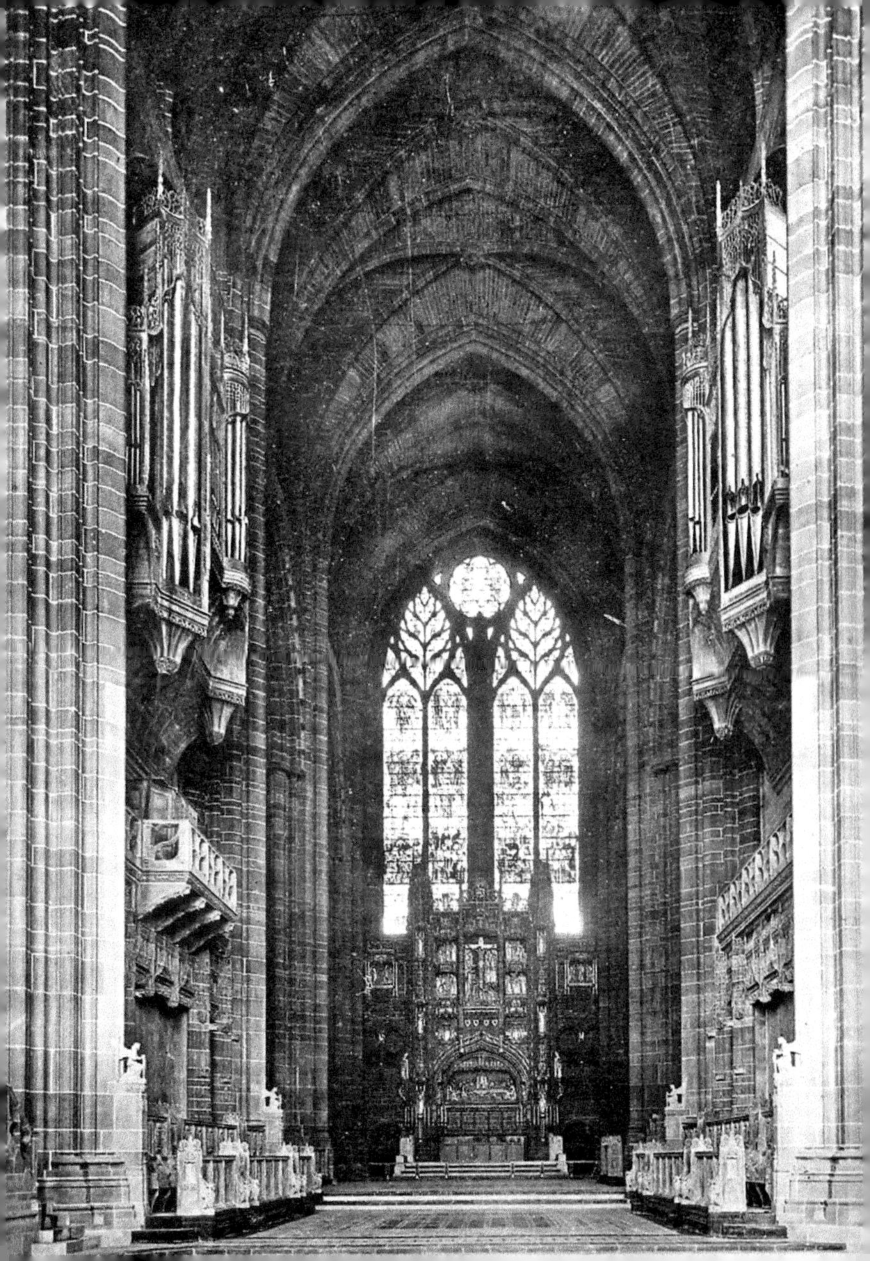

45. LIVERPOOL PHILHARMONIC HALL

The Liverpool Philharmonic Society was formed in 1840 and John Cunningham prepared plans for a concert hall in 1844. The foundation stone of the hall was laid in 1846 and it was completed in 1849 at a cost of £30,000. It was originally planned to build a hall with a capacity of 1,500 people but this was increased to accommodate an audience of 2,100, an orchestra of 250, and refreshment and retiring rooms. On 5 July 1933 the hall was destroyed by fire and Herbert J. Rowse was commissioned to design a new hall to be built on the same site. The new Philharmonic Hall was opened on 19 June 1939, with a concert conducted by Sir Thomas Beecham performed the following day. An extension was added to the rear of the hall in 1992 and it received a substantial refurbishment in 1995 at a cost of £10.3 million.

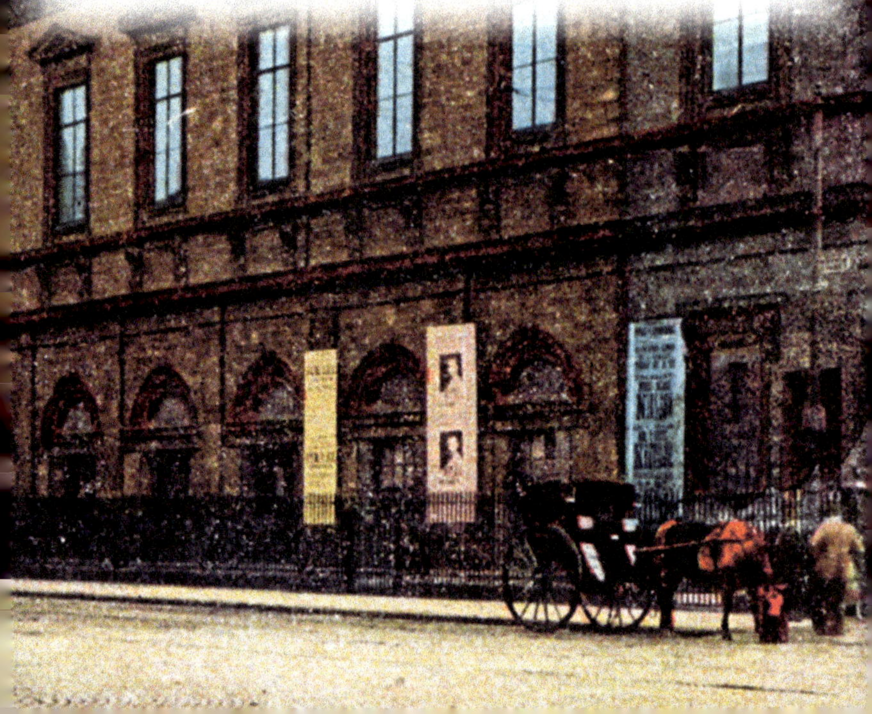

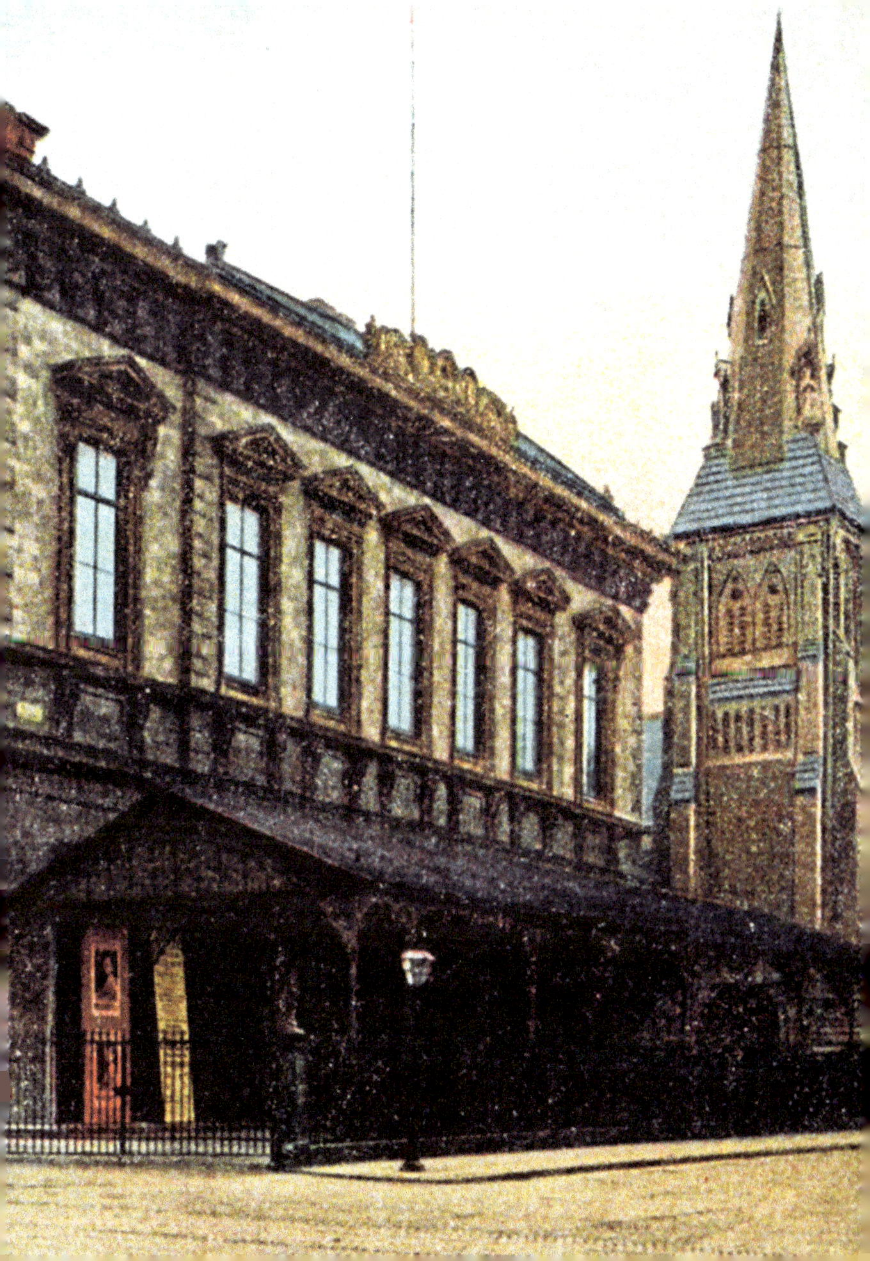

46. LIVERPOOL METROPOLITAN CATHEDRAL

The Metropolitan Cathedral was designed by Frederick Gibberd and was completed between 1962 and 1967. Richard Downey was appointed archbishop in 1928 and declared that he would build 'a cathedral in our time'. A 9-acre site in Mount Pleasant was acquired in 1930 and Edwin Lutyens was commissioned to design the new building. Lutyens proposed that the cathedral would be 680 feet long and 400 feet wide, with a dome of 168 feet, rising to 510 feet. It would have been larger than the Anglian Cathedral and St Peter's in Rome and would have been the second-largest church in the world. The Catholic Church soon realised that the scheme was becoming too large and expensive and Adrian Gilbert Scott looked at a smaller version of the building in 1955. However, a competition for a new design was announced in 1959, and it was specified that the building would be designed to allow closer involvement of the congregation of 2,000 worshipers, all in sight of the altar.

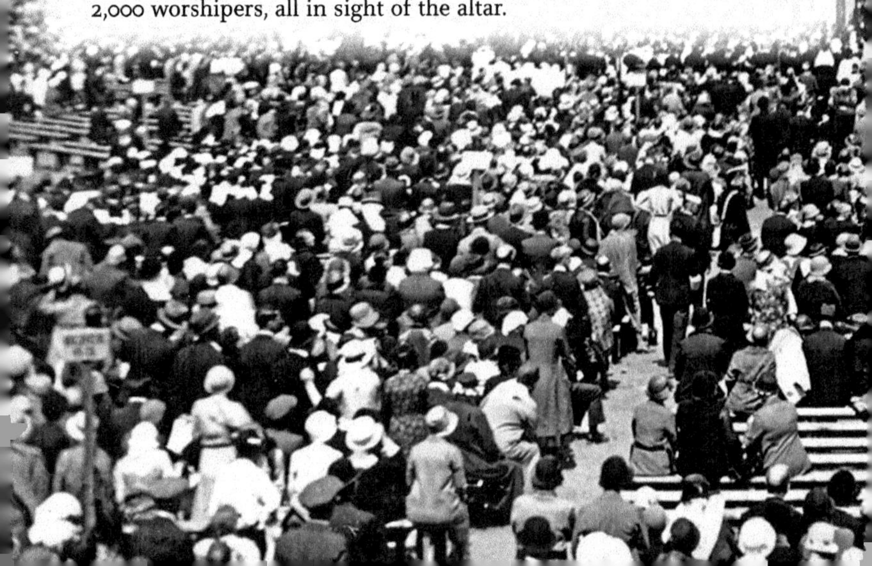

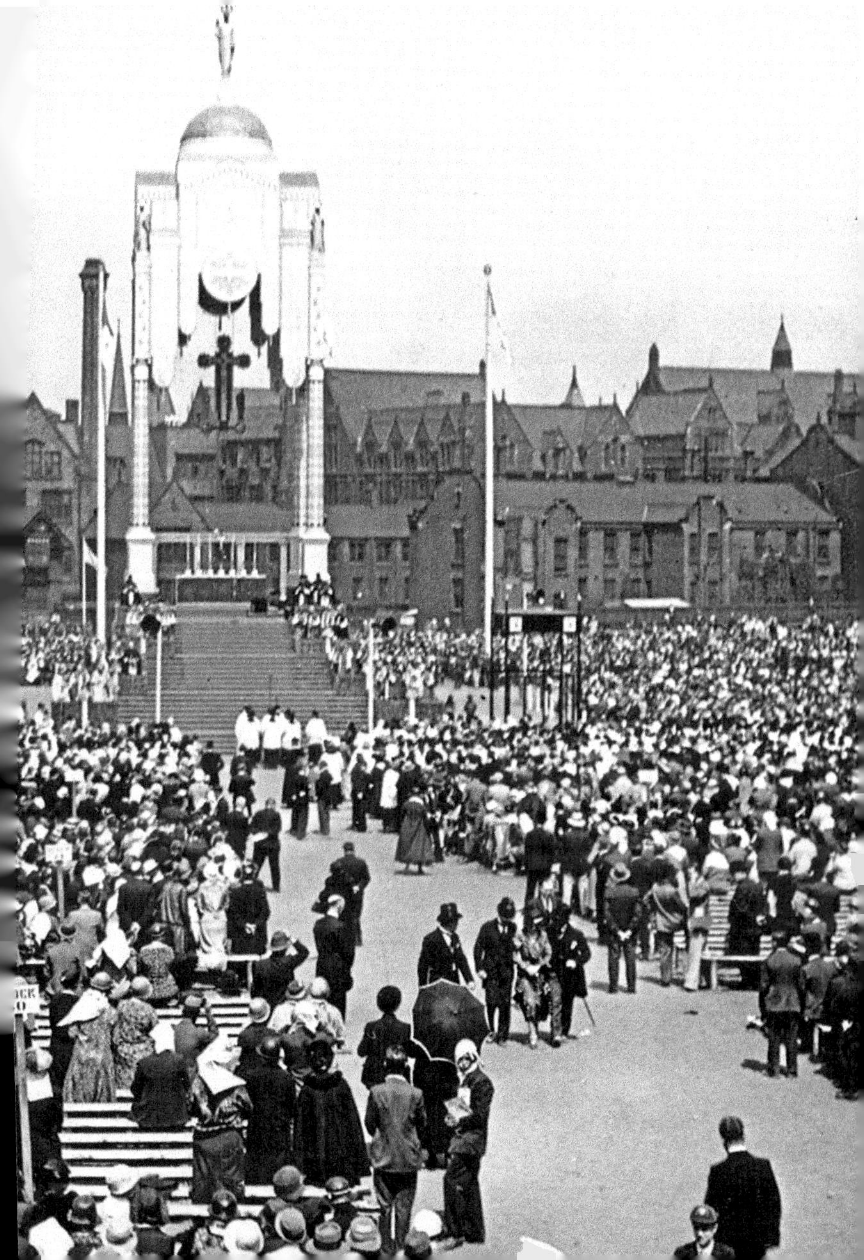

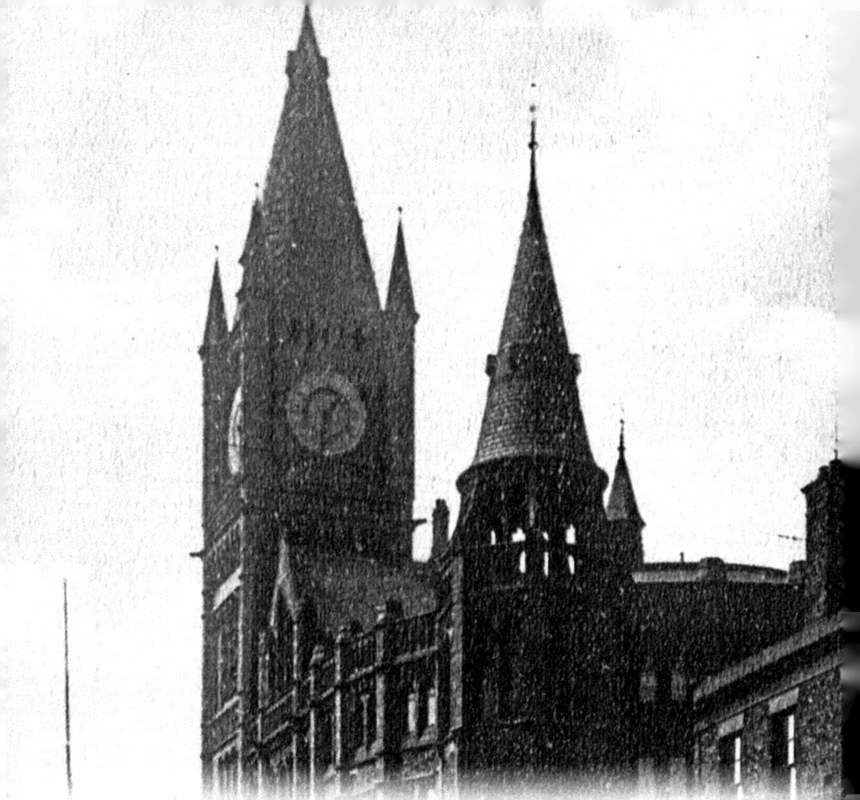

47. UNIVERSITY OF LIVERPOOL

University College Liverpool, founded by royal charter in 1881, was admitted into the Victoria University, Manchester, in 1884. The Victoria Building was completed between 1887 and 1892, and designed by Alfred Waterhouse to house University College before it became the University of Liverpool. In 1903, the University of Liverpool was established by royal charter and University College was absorbed into it. The college had ninety-three students, eleven professors and an income of £6,000. It is situated on the corner of Brownlow Hill and Ashton Street, and was built with accommodation for administration, teaching and also incorporates common rooms and a library.